BUY YOUR FREEDOM

From Waiting on Retirement to Freedom in Years, Not Decades

STERLING SEIZERT

Foreword by David Pere

SENTINEL RIDGE
PUBLISHING

Published by Sentinel Ridge Publishing

Jacksonville, Florida, USA

For permission requests, visit:

www.SterlingSeizert.com

ISBN: 979-8-89694-725-7 - Ebook

ISBN: 979-8-89694-726-4 - Paperback

Printed in the United States of America

Dedication

To my wife, thanks for the title suggestion. You're my rock. Your belief in me, even when I doubted myself, made this journey possible.

To my daughters, Sydney and Nora, this is for you. May you grow up knowing that you are never trapped, never limited, and always capable of building the life you want.

And to every man and woman who has served, sacrificed, and still found themselves stuck in a system that was never built for them, this book is your way out. Build your freedom. Change your legacy.

De Oppresso Liber
Sterling

Get the Tools to Fast-Track Your Freedom

Reading this book is just the beginning. To help you apply everything you'll learn and accelerate your journey to financial freedom, I've put together a collection of exclusive resources, completely free.

Scan the QR code or visit **SterlingSeizert.com/BookBonuses** to get instant access to:

- Step-by-step worksheets & checklists to map out your path to wealth
- Exclusive video lessons diving deeper into key strategies
- Templates to help you take action

You don't have to figure this out alone. These tools will help you take the next step with confidence. Grab them now and start building the life you actually want.

Scan Me

Join the Buy Your Freedom community free **Facebook group: Buy Your Freedom - Unconventional Wealth** for free tips and tricks and to start your journey with hundreds of others on the same journey.

Table of Contents

Part 5: Building Your Freedom Machine

Foreword

By David Pere

I joined the Marine Corps in 2008 and followed the same financial path as those before me. I spent my money on tattoos, cars, a beautiful new Harley Davidson motorcycle, alcohol. You name it.

In 2015, I was working 80+ hours a week on recruiting duty, and I felt trapped. It wasn't until somebody handed me a book and chastised me into actually reading it that I realized I could achieve financial freedom. Until that moment, I had fallen into the trap of "YOLO" and enjoying my money in the moment ...robbing myself of true freedom.

That book changed everything for me. In just over five years, I went from a negative net worth to a millionaire on paper, and more importantly, financially free. After 13 years of active service, I left the United States Marine Corps and haven't had to work a W-2 since.

Since then, as the founder of From Military to Millionaire, I've had a front-row seat to what separates the people who stay stuck from the people who break out, and it's not luck. It's clarity, ownership, and execution.

That's why Buy Your Freedom stood out to me early. One of Sterling's core frameworks, the Freedom Matrix, immediately caught my attention. It reminded me of Cashflow Quadrant, but felt cleaner, more actionable, and built for execution instead of theory. It was strong enough that both my COO and I independently texted Sterling about it before ever discussing the book together.

I've known Sterling for several years now. At first, I observed him on his self-storage investment journey from a distance as he participated in Facebook groups I was part of. Then he joined The War Room Mastermind, and I got to see him work and give back more closely. Most recently, I've had the pleasure of working with him directly, and I can tell you this: Sterling delivers.

His background as a Green Beret matters here, not as a flex, but because elite units are built on understanding terrain, identifying leverage points, and accounting for second-order effects before acting. That same Special Forces intel mindset shows up throughout this book. The frameworks aren't accidental. They're designed to help you see the system clearly before you move inside it.

That mindset has carried over into his investing and entrepreneurial pursuits, where he's consistently focused on ownership, systems, and outcomes rather than shortcuts or noise. What you're reading isn't theory or motivation—it's the product of a life spent operating in environments where clarity, preparation, and follow-through weren't optional.

It's rare to find someone operating in the wealth-building space who prioritizes systems, execution-driven, and long-term outcomes over flash, and that's why Sterling and I get along so well.

Buy Your Freedom is a clear, practical roadmap to financial freedom. It's framework-first and execu-tion-driven, written for people who actually want to change their situation, not just feel inspired for a week.

This book is for you if you've done everything "right", like getting a good job, steady paycheck, responsible choices, and you still feel trapped. You're not looking to "retire someday." You want freedom now: options, control, and income that doesn't disappear the second you stop working.

This book is not for you if you want the safe, traditional script: grind for 40 years, hope the market behaves, and pray you make it to 65. It's also not for anyone chasing shortcuts, hype, or imaginary "passive income." This book is about doing the real work of building assets, leverage, and ownership, so you stop trading your life for permission.

You don't need me to tell you to read this book; you already picked it up.

What you do need is to do what most people won't: finish it and implement it.

Because the only thing worse than being stuck is staying stuck on purpose.

–David Pere, Founder, From Military to Millionaire

INTRODUCTION

The System Isn't What You Think

It's 2013. I'm stuck in traffic outside Fort Carson, Colorado, staring at a sea of brake lights stretching into the distance. Same commute. Same routine. Same life on repeat.

Drive. Work. Drive. Sleep. Repeat. I could see the next thirty years in those brake lights.

By that point I was seven years into what would become a twelve-year Army career. I was a Green Beret. I'd operated in some of the most complex environments on the planet. And sitting there in that traffic jam, I realized something that hit harder than any operation I'd been a part of.

I was a soldier. And when I got out, I'd basically still be one. Just for a company instead of a country.

Swap the uniform for a polo shirt. Swap the commander for a boss. Same structure. Someone else owns your schedule. Someone else decides what your time is worth. Someone else holds the power to keep you or cut you loose.

Every worker is just a soldier. Same deal: trade your time, follow the program, and hope the system keeps its promises.

That morning I decided that when I walked away from the Army, I wasn't going to walk into the same structure with a different name. I didn't want to be a Worker. I wanted to be an Owner.

I didn't know the full picture yet. But I knew the question that would guide everything from that point forward: Am I saving like a Worker, or building like an Owner?

I was frustrated because, on paper, I had done everything "right." Seven years of active duty. Three deployments. A stable paycheck. A house. Security. But I'm not free. The financial stress never fully goes away.

I remember my wife and I first starting out, eating ramen and hard-boiled eggs, sleeping on a borrowed air mattress, and stretching $650 paychecks to cover $850 rent. I promised myself we'd never live like that again. And we didn't.

But getting out of survival mode didn't mean I had it figured out. I overspent. I upgraded too fast. I made the kind of financial mistakes that look normal from the outside but keep you stuck on the inside.

Years later, after a few promotions and raises, life looked better: nicer cars, bigger house, higher income, a little savings. But sitting there in traffic, I realized something uncomfortable.

The problems had changed shape but hadn't disappeared. We still worried about money. Still worried about time. Still worried about what would happen if something broke, someone got sick, or the system shifted.

And that's when the thought hit me, clean and simple: *In a brutally practical way, almost all the pain, problems, and pressures in our lives came down to the same shortages.*

Not enough time.

Not enough money.

Not enough control.

I felt trapped.

Researchers have studied what actually makes people happy. It's not money. It's agency. The feeling that you control your own life. Yet here I was, doing everything right, with none of it.

I always get a kick out of people who say, "Money doesn't buy happiness." They say it like it's some enlightened truth. But if you hand them a hundred bucks, they'll smile. Every time.

Take any couple. Same love. Same values. Same commitment. Cut their income in half.

Every bill gets heavy. Every purchase becomes a discussion. Every surprise becomes a crisis. Not because they love each other less, but because stress narrows people and shrinks patience.

Now double their income. Bills are automatic. Emergencies are inconvenient, but not catastrophic. Same relationship. Completely different emotional environment. Now give them more time too. No mandatory commute. No choosing between work and family when something goes wrong.

Money didn't create the love. It removed the weight crushing it. That's what financial freedom actually buys. Not yachts, watches, or status. Options, time, and control. The ability to pursue a deeply personal mission you chose instead of one assigned by a payroll system. It's not escaping work. It's taking ownership of what your work, time, and money are in service of.

That morning in traffic, it all clicked. I didn't rage. I didn't spiral. I just sat there and admitted a truth I'd been avoiding: "*I can't do this for another 30 years. I want different. I want more. I want freedom.*"

That was my new mission. What scared me wasn't failure or learning how. It was the repetition every day, the fear of staying the same. The idea of living the next three decades exactly like the last seven years felt worse than any uncertainty I could imagine.

What I didn't understand yet was that nothing was actually "wrong" with me. I wasn't lazy. I wasn't reckless. I wasn't bad with money. I was doing exactly what I'd been conditioned to do: optimize for stability, minimize risk, and be responsible.

The problem was that I was unconsciously optimizing for safety inside a system that could never deliver the freedom I wanted. I was aiming at the wrong target.

I came to realize there's a trap almost everyone falls into. A model that looks responsible, feels safe, and is socially rewarded, but structurally keeps you dependent.

I call it the Accumulation Trap: the belief that if you save long enough, invest responsibly enough, and wait patiently enough, freedom will eventually arrive. It's the default script. It's what everyone around you follows. It's the system that keeps Workers working, where they benefit last from their own effort and their own money, if they benefit at all.

The Accumulation Trap doesn't care how hard you work. It doesn't care how disciplined you are. It teaches you to keep accumulating so that one day you can retire, which means you have to keep working, keep complying, and keep postponing your life in the meantime. It quietly trades control for permission. It's the financial system's version of "hurry up and wait."

That was the moment I stopped being a Worker and started building like an Owner.

I began studying money, wealth, and financial freedom the way I had been trained by the military to study threat networks, environments, and battlefields, by looking at how things actually worked, not how they were marketed. Not what people say on television, but what people who owned their time and income were doing in real life. What I found changed everything for my family.

Why I Wrote This Book

I didn't write this book because I got lucky or struck it rich overnight. I wrote it because I was stuck in that traffic jam and I found a way out. I found freedom.

One year after that morning, I closed my first deal: an 18-unit apartment building in Colorado Springs for $900,000. The down payment was $300,000. I negotiated seller financing on the balance at 5%.

I was excited and scared all at once. I only had $3,000 to my name. I didn't have the money, but I had learned to ask a better question: How can I make this work?

I shared the deal with everyone I knew in the local investor community. I showed the numbers. Two people, essentially strangers, funded the down payment. One used a self-directed IRA. The other used cash sitting idle. They brought the capital. I brought the deal and the work.

For the first time in my life, I owned an asset that paid me whether I showed up or not. Eighteen units. Eighteen tenants. Eighteen checks every month. That was my turning point because it revealed something fundamental: income tied to ownership behaves very differently than income tied to labor.

Real estate happened to be my vehicle, but this book is not about real estate. It's about ownership. The mechanics apply whether you're buying an apartment building, a car wash, a service business, or some other income-producing assets.

Soon after, my wife took a different path. She started a service company with $2,000. Within a year, it was netting her $4,000-$5,000 monthly. Different asset class. Same principle: ownership that produces income.

We kept building from there. Eventually, our assets gave us something most people never get: options.

In late 2021, I was working as a military contractor making $98,000 a year. Then the vaccine mandate came down. Comply or lose your job.

That day I drove home nervously to find my wife sitting in the garage on a camping chair watching our daughters color the driveway with chalk. I broke the news and we talked through the risks and our choices. Our family has a heart health history, so for us, the risk was not something we were willing to accept.

What made that conversation different from the ones happening all around us was simple. We had a choice. Our assets were already generating $8,500 per month. Enough to replace my paycheck.

My wife looked at me and said, "If you don't have to comply, then don't."

We had already built the income, so I had the choice. I walked away. I was 39.

It pained me watching my brothers, men who fought and bled for their country, with no options but to comply. They had families to feed, mortgages to pay, kids in school.

They didn't lack courage. They lacked options. Their paycheck was used as leverage to force a decision they would not have made freely.

What I saw in that moment was the true cost of financial dependence. When your income is controlled by others, your choices are never fully your own. That paycheck was my employer's leverage.

That's the quiet power of money. And that's exactly what financial freedom removes.

Financial freedom is not about retiring at 65 or escaping to a beach. It is about having options when life corners you. It is about being able to say no.

Today, my assets generate much more than $8,500 per month. I work on my self-storage business on my terms, some weeks five hours, some weeks thirty. I'm not retired, sitting on a recliner watching TV. And I don't want to be. I'm 42 and I get to do what I want, when I want, with whomever I want. My time belongs to me and my family. That's the difference.

The Mission

As I was working to become financially free, I spent over a decade in U.S. Army Special Forces, the Green Berets. We specialize in unconventional warfare, where understanding systems and people is critical to the mission.

I wasn't just a shooter. I was the Intelligence Sergeant. My job was to understand the environment, the systems that shaped it, and how pressure applied in the right place created second and third order effects.

Our motto is *De Oppresso Liber*: to free the oppressed.

The same methodology I used to understand and operate inside political and human systems overseas, I applied to financial systems at home. We can't operate effectively inside any system until we understand how it actually works: the incentives, the players, the invisible rules. This book is about understanding that terrain first.

I'm not one of those financial "gurus" who got rich selling advice they never actually used to get where they are. I won't ask you to do anything I haven't done. I built my freedom and wealth by learning the concepts and applying the very strategies I'm about to share with you.

More than anything, I'm passionate about helping others find their way out. If I can get free, so can you.

What This Book Will Give You

This isn't another personal finance book telling you to save your way to retirement at 65. It's not about budgeting harder, investing in index funds, and hoping compound interest saves you in three or four decades.

This is for people who don't want to spend the next 20-40 years working a job. This is for people who want to own their time and control their outcomes, not wait until they're too old to enjoy it.

You'll learn:

- Why conventional retirement planning breaks down mathematically

- How income behaves differently at each stage
- How assets create freedom while labor creates ceilings
- Why leverage and ownership matter more than frugality
- How to start even if you don't have much money.

This is the "what" and the "why" of the system you are operating in. The mechanics and specific tactics come later. Once you understand how money actually moves, the "how" becomes much more obvious and far easier to execute.

The Frameworks Behind the Freedom

Real estate and real estate-centric businesses were my vehicle, but they weren't the secret. The principles in this book apply far beyond any single asset class. Whether you build through real estate, businesses, or other income-producing assets, the structure underneath is the same.

Think of what comes next as your financial freedom intelligence briefing. We'll study the terrain and identify the forces at play. You'll understand the incentives, the choke points, and the paths of movement. Only then can you choose your course of action toward freedom.

That's what these frameworks are. Mental models to make sense of reality. They let you see the likely outcome of any financial path before you take it. They show you where freedom is created, where it's lost, and where leverage actually exists. They give you the map before you're asked to make decisions that will shape the next 10, 20, or 30 years of your life.

Every income source and every asset can be understood through two primary variables:

- how much time it requires
- how much control and leverage it provides.

From that structure came two core frameworks.

The *Five Stages of Income* explains where your money comes from and why some people work harder every year yet feel more trapped, while others build income that compounds and eventually replaces their labor.

The *Freedom Matrix* shows how assets behave over time. Whether they create freedom or dependency. Whether they compound your effort or consume it. Whether they build options or quietly take them away.

I use some real estate examples throughout this book because that's my deepest experience. But I've helped friends and family apply the same concepts and frameworks in completely different arenas. I'll show you their stories too, like one friend who bought an HVAC company with seller financing and climbed from salary to semi-passive business income in under three years. Different asset. Same frameworks. Same result.

Let's Go

This book started as conversations with friends, colleagues, and family over coffee, in parking lots, and after long days when they asked how I was doing what I was doing and why I didn't follow conventional advice. This book is those conversations, written down.

What follows isn't a rant or a theory. It's a cause-and-effect breakdown of why the system rewards dependence and delays ownership, and how to build around it.

Once you see how it works, you can't unsee it. The old rules stop making sense.

If you're done trading your life for permission, turn the page.

PART 1

Everything You Were Taught About Money Is Wrong

CHAPTER 1

Retirement - The Broken Plan That Fails Most People

My dad did everything right.

Naval Academy graduate. Nuclear engineer. Teacher. A great and impactful man. He didn't buy fancy cars. Didn't take extravagant vacations. Saved diligently. Followed every piece of traditional financial advice.

His dream was simple: retire comfortably, travel, enjoy some well-earned rest after decades of hard work.

He retired at 64. One year later, he was gone.

One. Fucking. Year.

That's all he got after a lifetime of sacrifice.

I think about that every time someone tells me to "save for retirement" and "enjoy it later." Later isn't guaranteed. And the model most people follow doesn't just delay life. It trades your best years for a paycheck and calls it success.

Time is the ultimate currency. The traditional retirement model spends it first.

The Accumulation Trap

As Thomas Sowell wrote, "Many beliefs which collapse under scrutiny may nevertheless persist indefinitely when they are not scrutinized, and especially when skilled advocates are able to perpetuate those beliefs by forestalling scrutiny through appeals to emotions or interests."[20]

The Accumulation Trap is one of those beliefs. Let's scrutinize it.

For most of my life, I followed the script: work hard, go to school, land the job, buy the house, save for retirement. On the surface, it felt responsible. Underneath, it's a model built on sacrifice and hope.

The traditional model has a name: the Accumulation Model.

Here's how it works: work hard for 40 years, save as much as you can, pile up a nest egg big enough to slowly spend down once you stop working.

It's built on a fundamental assumption: sacrifice enjoyment from the money you're earning today to stash it into retirement accounts you can't touch for decades, then take it all out later to live on.

Live below your means. Delay the fun. Skip the vacations. Be responsible. If you're lucky, you get to stop working sometime in your 60s and hope you don't outlive your savings.

That's the model. I call it the Accumulation Trap. Now let's look at the math.

The 4% Rule: The Default Retirement Plan

The financial industry built a model to calculate your "magic number" for retirement. The most famous version is called the 4% Rule.

The idea is simple: withdraw 4% of your retirement savings in your first year of retirement, then adjust for inflation each year after. If all goes well, your money should last about 30 years.[16]

To figure out your number, decide how much income you want in retirement and multiply by 25.

- Save $1 million, withdraw about $40,000 the first year.
- Save $2 million, withdraw about $80,000 before taxes.
- Save $2.5 million, withdraw $100,000.

Sounds reasonable until you ask: How is the average person supposed to save $2 million?

Let's run the numbers. The S&P 500 has averaged roughly 10% nominal return annually since 1926, but over the last 25 years it's been closer to 7.5%. Using 8% for planning, to hit $2 million by age 65 you'd need to save $600 per month for 40 years, or $1,350 per month for 30 years.[16]

That's over $16,000 less per year to live on. For decades. While you're raising kids, paying off student loans, and trying to enjoy life while you're still young.

That's not saving. That's selling your healthiest decades to buy back your weakest ones. Plus, your odds of getting to enjoy them aren't guaranteed.

Even if you hit that magic number, the model has three fatal flaws.

Fatal Flaw #1: Underestimating Future Costs

In 1995, TIAA-CREF ran a print ad warning people about future costs. It predicted that in thirty years:

- A burger and fries could cost $16
- A vacation could cost $12,500
- A basic car could cost $65,000

The tagline: "No problem. You'll eat in. You won't drive. And you won't go anywhere."

In 1995, those numbers sounded absurd. A burger and fries were $3 to $5.

But we're living in that future now. At many restaurants, a burger and fries is right around $16. A family vacation can easily run $12,000 or more.

I remember this from my own childhood. In the early 1990s, I could walk into a convenience store and buy a candy bar and a 20-ounce

Mountain Dew for about $1.50. Today, that same purchase runs four or five bucks without blinking.

That's exactly how the 1995 investor felt when someone told them a burger would someday cost $16. If you're thinking "I need $60,000 a year to retire comfortably," you're probably thinking in today's dollars. At historical inflation rates, a $16 burger today costs $50 in 30 years.[21]

Sounds ridiculous. So did $16 in 1995.

In 20 years, you'll need $120,000 to match the purchasing power of $60,000 today. In 30 years, you'll need about $168,000.[7,8]

But retirees don't experience "average" inflation. They get hit where it hurts:

- Healthcare spending per person has exploded
- Property taxes and insurance keep rising even after the mortgage is paid
- Roofs, HVAC systems, and cars wear out on fixed incomes
- Food and services inflate faster than the CPI

The Accumulation Trap assumes you can predict all of this decades in advance. But real life isn't average. And the costs that dominate retirement rise faster than most plans assume.

Fatal Flaw #2: Taxes on the Crop, Not the Seed

You've been told saving in a traditional IRA and 401(k) is smart. Here's what most people don't account for: the government taxes that money when you withdraw it, like regular income from a job.[12]

The entire model assumes you'll be living on less when you retire, so you'll be in a lower tax bracket. But what if you don't want to live on less?

Say you've saved $2 million and withdraw $80,000 a year. The IRS sees that the same as if you earned $80,000 from a job. At current tax rates, after federal taxes that may look more like the mid-$60Ks. Before state taxes.

By deferring taxes, you didn't save money. You deferred into a worse deal. You're paying taxes on the crop, not just the seed.

And if tax rates increase, it gets worse. The bet is that your future tax rate will be lower. That's uncertain at best.

This isn't an argument to ignore retirement accounts. It's an argument to not rely on them as your primary freedom strategy.

Fatal Flaw #3: Longevity and Timing Risk

The 4% Rule is designed to make your money last about 30 years. But what if you want to retire earlier? What if you live longer? What if you retire at 65 and live to 100?

And what if the market crashes in your first few years of retirement?[5]

We've been assuming a consistent 8% return, but markets fluctuate wildly. Some years you're up 20%. Some years you're down 20%. If those down years hit early in retirement, the math falls apart.

If you're withdrawing while the market is down, you're selling shares at the worst possible time. That damage compounds. This is called sequence of returns risk.[16]

A 20% loss doesn't require a 20% gain to recover. It requires a 25% gain just to get back to even. Before you've withdrawn a single dollar to live on.

The model assumes average returns, average longevity, and average timing. Real lives have ups and downs.

What the Numbers Actually Look Like

Let me show you what happens when you follow the traditional advice perfectly.

You're making $100,000 per year. About $8,300 per month. You follow every rule. You do everything "right." You save 15% of your income, $1,250 per month, into your 401(k).

After taxes and deductions, you're down to about $5,700 take-home to pay for housing, utilities, student loans, food, children, and everything else.

Fast forward 30 years.

You've saved around $1.86 million, assuming 8% returns, no lost decades, no mistimed crashes, no major planning errors.

Using the 4% Rule, that generates about $74,000 in your first year of retirement. After taxes, closer to $5,000 per month. Add Social Security and you're at roughly $7,000 per month in future dollars.

After adjusting those future dollars back into today's buying power, that spends like $2,500 to $2,900 per month.

After three decades of work, disciplined saving, and perfect execution, the system delivers the equivalent of about $30,000 to $35,000 per year in today's buying power.

That's planning to live on a tight budget in retirement. And that's if everything goes as planned. That's your reward for 30+ years of discipline and sacrifice.

And before you think, "this doesn't apply to me because my employer matches," or "my spouse works too," let's steelman the best case.

Say your employer matches dollar for dollar up to 6% of your salary. That adds $500 per month to your $1,250 contribution. After 30 years at 8%, your nest egg grows to about $2.6 million instead of $1.8 million. Your 4% withdrawal jumps to about $104,000 per year. After federal and state taxes, roughly $7,000 per month. Add Social Security and you're at about $8,900 per month in future dollars. In today's purchasing power? About $3,200 to $3,700 per month. Better. Still not freedom.

Now let's even add a spouse with both of you earning $100,000. Both saving 15%. Both getting the full match. Both executing perfectly for 30 years. Combined nest egg: roughly $5.2 million. Combined income with Social Security: about $17,800 per month in future dollars. In today's purchasing power, that's about $6,400 to $7,400 per month combined. Call it $75,000 to $88,000 per year between two people.

That's the best-case version of the Accumulation Model. Two six-figure earners, full employer match, 30 years each, zero mistakes, no layoffs, perfect execution.

But, most households don't have two six-figure earners. Most don't get a full 6% match. Most can't save 15% for three decades without interruption. And even the ones who can, who do everything right, end up here. Not broke. But not free either. Sixty years of combined labor, perfect execution, and the reward is splitting the equivalent of $7,000 a month and hoping the furnace doesn't die.

The Numbers Most People Never Hit

Using the 4% Rule, $10,000 a month in retirement income requires roughly $3 million saved.

The reality:

- Only 0.8% of Americans have $3 million saved
- Only 1.8% have $2 million
- Only 4.7% have $1 million

And roughly 80% of households near retirement are economically insecure.[18,19]

The model isn't failing because people lack discipline. It's failing because the math doesn't work.

What "Success" Actually Looks Like

I know a couple who did everything right. Both worked full careers. Saved consistently. Retired in their mid-sixties with about $800,000, which felt like a lot at the time.

Ten years in, they're watching every dollar. His Medicare premiums jumped. Her prescriptions went up. Their car died and they financed a replacement at 7%. They stopped taking the grandkids on trips. Not because they don't want to. Because they don't trust the math.

They're not poor, but they're not free either. They traded 40 years for this. And now they're afraid to spend what they saved because they don't know how long it has to last.

My dad never really experienced retirement. This couple made it. Neither outcome looks like freedom to me.

The Backwards Logic

Step back and look at what you're being sold.

Spend 30 to 40 years building a pile of money. Then spend the next 30 years slowly draining it, hoping you guessed right on inflation, taxes, timing, and how long you live.

That's backwards.

If the goal is income, build income.

Instead of saving millions to someday buy freedom, build or buy assets that pay you now and keep paying you.

One freedom asset netting $1,000 a month changes your breathing. It covers a car payment. It creates margin. It gives you options.

Then you scale. One thousand becomes five. Five becomes ten. Ten becomes twenty. No need to wait till 65. You stop waiting for retirement and start building it.

If your income only exists while you're working, nothing fundamental has changed. You've just delayed the problem.

The Choice

The real question isn't "When do I retire?"

It's "When does my asset income cover my life?"

The Accumulation Trap trades 40 years of labor for replacement income in your 60s. The math requires it. Inflation guarantees it. Taxes confirm it. The outcome is not freedom. It's dependence.

Most people never run the numbers honestly, so they never realize this is the trade they're making. They think they're choosing security. What they're actually choosing is delayed life: sacrificing their healthiest, most energetic years to a system built on delay and dependence.

If you follow the default path, you are making a bet. You're betting your best years on things you can't control: market returns, tax policy, inflation, government promises, and how long you live.

If you reject that path, you are not being reckless. You are choosing agency instead of hope. You are choosing a different model entirely.

Instead of saving money to someday turn it into income, you build income first. Instead of hoping your money lasts, you create cash flow that doesn't depend on perfect timing or slow spend-down.

Financial freedom is not an age or a number in an account. It's an income level: the moment the income from your assets cover your life.

The question isn't whether you'll choose.

The question is whether you'll choose by default or by design.

Cause and Effect

What you just saw isn't a coincidence. It's not bad luck. And it's not because most people are irresponsible or undisciplined.

A system doesn't produce the same outcome for tens of millions of people by accident.

The Accumulation Model wasn't designed around your freedom. It was designed around stability, control, and predictable capital flows for the system itself. For the institutions, not individuals.

When you understand who designed it, who benefits from it, and how the incentives are structured, the entire retirement narrative flips.

What you just saw is the effect. The math doesn't work. The risk is on you. The outcome is dependence on employers, markets, the government, and the system.

Those aren't random results. They're the logical output of a system built a certain way.

In the next chapter, we stop looking at outcomes and start looking at causes. We follow the money.

CHAPTER 2

Follow the Money: How the System Was Built

"All Currencies devalue or die, and when they do, cash and bonds (which are promises to receive currency) are devalued or wiped out."

—*Ray Dalio, The Changing World Order*

Nobody satisfactorily explained any of this to me until I was in my thirties.

I did everything I was supposed to do. Worked hard. Saved. Put money in my 401(k). And every year, I felt like I was running on a treadmill that kept speeding up. Prices rose faster than my raises. My savings account balance grew, but its purchasing power didn't. I was following the rules and falling behind.

Then I started reading. Not the mainstream personal finance advice. The stuff behind it. Federal Reserve policy. Monetary history. Tax code structure. The origins of the 401(k).

And the more I learned, the angrier I got.

Not because I'd made mistakes. Because what I'd been taught by school, by financial advisors, by well-meaning family didn't fit reality. It directly contradicted it. The rules I'd been following were not designed to make me free. They were designed to make me useful in the system. Useful to employers. Useful to Wall Street. Useful to the government.

The system isn't broken. It's working exactly as it's designed. Just not for people like me. And likely not for people like you either.

Chapter 1 showed you the math doesn't work. The Accumulation Trap fails most people. Not because they're bad with money, but because the model itself is flawed.

Now let's answer two questions: Why did this become the default plan? And who benefits when you spend 40 years accumulating instead of owning?

This is systems analysis. The raw intel on how the financial terrain got shaped before you ever entered it.

Let's follow the money.

The Pension Shift: How Retirement Risk Got Transferred to You

The Accumulation Model didn't exist 50 years ago. Your grandparents didn't need to save for retirement the way you're told to. Most had pensions.

Under the traditional pension system, employers guaranteed retirees a percentage of their working salary for life. The company bore the investment risk, the longevity risk, and the inflation risk. You worked for them for 30 years, you retired, and you received a predictable monthly check until you died.

That model worked well for employees. It worked less well for corporate balance sheets.

In 1974, Congress passed ERISA. The stated goal was protecting workers. The actual effect was making pensions more expensive and complex to maintain. Over the following decades, companies moved away from guaranteed pensions and toward defined contribution plans like the 401(k).[4]

The 401(k) started as a supplemental savings vehicle for high earners. It quickly became the default retirement plan for everyone else.[4]

Under the old model, the company guaranteed your income, managed the investments, and shouldered the risk. Under the new model, you do all three.

The pitch was empowerment. "Take control of your retirement." The system didn't eliminate risk. It quietly dumped it on you and called it "personal responsibility."

Who benefits? Corporations shed expensive pension liabilities for predictable, limited contributions with no long-term obligation. Wall Street collects fees on trillions in retirement assets, turning your retirement into their revenue stream. Government defers tax collection while locking capital in the market.[3]

And you? You fund it, manage it, and hope it works out.

The 401(k) is a risk-transfer mechanism wrapped in a tax benefit.

So, avoid it? No. Use it up to the employer match. Just don't depend on it as your freedom strategy.

How Inflation Actually Works

The Accumulation Model assumes your dollars will hold their value. They won't.

The U.S. monetary system is managed by the Federal Reserve, established in 1913. The Fed operates under a dual mandate: maximize employment and stabilize prices. In practice, it uses tools that systematically favor asset holders over wage earners.[9,10]

Here's how it works. When the government spends more than it collects, it borrows by issuing Treasury bonds. The Federal Reserve buys those bonds, pumping new money into the financial system. Over time, sustained expansion of the money and credit leads to prices increasing faster than wages grow.

In this system, moderate inflation is intentional, as Ray Dalio pointed out. It reduces the real burden of government debt over time. The government repays yesterday's obligations with tomorrow's cheaper dollars.

The borrower benefits. Savers absorb the cost through lost purchasing power. But timing matters too.

New money enters the economy at specific points. The government spends it first. Banks lend it next. Asset prices rise before consumer prices adjust. By the time new money reaches wage earners through salary increases, prices have already moved higher.

This is called the Cantillon Effect, named after 18th-century economist Richard Cantillon. Those closest to money creation benefit first and most. Those furthest away, people trading time for wages, pay the price through eroded purchasing power.[11]

Your raises never catch up to prices. They're not supposed to.

The Gold Standard and What Changed

This wasn't the first time the government changed the rules to protect the system at the expense of citizens. In 1933, Roosevelt signed Executive Order 6102, making it illegal for Americans to hold gold and forcing them to sell to the government at $20.67 per ounce. The government then revalued gold to $35—a 41% overnight wealth transfer from citizens to the U.S. Treasury.

Forty years later, Nixon finished the job. In 1971, President Nixon ended the dollar's convertibility to gold, removing the last external constraint on U.S. money creation.[6]

The impact was dramatic. From 1920 to 1970, consumer prices roughly doubled over fifty years. Since the early 1970s, prices have risen about eightfold over a similar span.[7]

You can see this in almost anything that matters.

In 1971, the median home price was about $25,000. Today it's over $400,000. In 1971, a year of public college tuition averaged around $500. Today it's closer to $11,000. The minimum wage in 1971 was $1.60. If it had kept pace with true inflation, it would be well over $15 today, and that's using conservative measures.[3,7,8]

The dollars you save today will not buy the same life in 20 years. The system guarantees it.

Many forces influence inflation. But removing the gold standard eliminated the main constraint on how many dollars the government could create.

The result: Prices rise. Asset values inflate. The wealth gap widens. Stock portfolios, real estate, and businesses grow faster than wages.

The system rewards those who own assets. Not those who only earn income.

In an inflationary system, saving dollars is a losing strategy. Asset ownership is the winning one.

The Tax Code Rewards Ownership, Punishes Labor

The same year the Federal Reserve was created, 1913, the 16th Amendment established federal income tax.[12]

Originally, income tax applied only to the wealthiest Americans, about 1% of the population. The rates were low. The promise was it would never expand to the working class.

Today, the average W-2 employee is the government's most reliable revenue source and the easiest to collect from. The money is taken before you ever see it.

The tax code is nearly 7,000 pages long. Most of it isn't restrictions. It's incentives. And those incentives reward ownership and investment, not labor.

When you're a W-2 employee, you earn income, the government takes its share immediately through withholding. You pay taxes on gross income, and you live on what's left.

When you're a business owner or investor, you earn income, deduct business expenses, reinvest profits, and pay taxes on what's left.

The difference is structural. We'll break this down in full in Chapter 15.

The tax code incentivizes ownership and penalizes trading time for wages.

Two people earning the same amount can end up with completely different lives.

Why The Rules Changed

Your grandparents could work one job and retire comfortably. Pensions guaranteed income. Companies bore the risk. The dollar was constrained by gold. The economy rewarded stability.

Today, pensions are gone and you bear all the risk. Inflation is structural. The dollar has no external constraint. The tax code favors ownership over labor.

The 401(k) shift transferred retirement risk to individuals while creating recurring revenue for Wall Street. Inflation erodes the purchasing power of saved dollars while rewarding those who own appreciating assets. The tax structure extracts heavily from labor while incentivizing ownership and investment.

These aren't separate problems. They're one system.

The system isn't broken. It works exactly as designed. It rewards ownership, leverage, and proximity to capital creation. It extracts from labor, savings, and delayed consumption.

Once you see it, you can't unsee it.

You have two options.

Option 1: The default path. Trade time for wages. Save in dollars that lose purchasing power. Defer taxes into an unknown future. Carry all the risk yourself. Hope the math works out.

Option 2: Build around how the system actually works. Acquire assets that produce income and appreciate with inflation. Use the tax code as it's designed. Build freedom in years, not decades.

What does that freedom actually look like? Slow mornings with your kids instead of rushing out the door. Taking a couple weeks off without asking permission. Handling a broken car or medical bill without financial panic. Not checking your retirement account every time the market drops, wondering if you'll ever stop working. Building something that's yours instead of renting your time to someone else's vision.

The rest of this book is about Option 2. But before you can build differently, you have to think differently. The system didn't just shape your finances. It shaped your beliefs about money. That's where we start.

PART 2

Financial Freedom Starts in Your Mind

CHAPTER 3

Identify Your Money Beliefs

Before you can master money, you have to master your mind about money.

I didn't realize how true this was until I watched myself sabotage my own progress. Repeatedly.

Every time I saved or invested, I felt loss, not progress. I remember finally saving $3,000. Instead of pride, my chest tightened. My brain didn't see opportunity. It saw deprivation. Things I'd earned but couldn't spend.

That wasn't logic. That was programming.

Your money beliefs aren't just thoughts. They're survival mechanisms shaped by family, culture, and experiences you didn't choose.

Maybe you grew up hearing "rich people are greedy" or "money causes problems." Maybe you watched financial stress tear relationships apart. Maybe you lived in a neighborhood where just getting by was a victory and wealth felt distant, or even suspicious.

These beliefs didn't come from nowhere. They were installed for a reason: to help you survive the world you were growing up in.

The problem is that survival strategies don't build wealth. They keep you safe. They keep you small.

The Paradigm: Your Internal Operating System

We all see money through a paradigm: a set of beliefs, assumptions, fears, and expectations running every financial decision we make.

Your paradigm is your unique mix of knowledge, experience, and faith or fear. It becomes your automatic filter. The lens through which you see the world. It decides what feels "normal," what feels "dangerous," what feels "possible," and what feels "out of reach."

I didn't examine any of this for years. I didn't know why investing felt risky. I didn't know why I felt guilty wanting more. I didn't know why opportunity made me freeze. I just assumed that's how I was wired.

I was wrong. I wasn't wired that way. I was programmed that way. There's a difference.

You Cannot Outperform Your Paradigm

You can get inspired for a moment, but you'll always snap back to your default programming when pressure hits.

Your paradigm is a thermostat. Try to rise above it, and you'll unconsciously sabotage yourself back to the level you feel safe at.

This is why people read financial books, take courses, start budgets, try new strategies, and still end up right back where they were. They tried to change their actions without first changing their operating system.

Mine showed up in a boring, predictable way. Every time I had a good month or built a little momentum, I'd "reward" myself by eating out a few extra times or making small impulse buys. Nothing reckless. Just enough to slide right back to where I felt normal.

That wasn't discipline failing. That was my thermostat pulling me back.

To transform your financial life, you must first identify the beliefs that shaped your paradigm. Not to judge them. Not to shame yourself. But to reveal the invisible script running your life without your permission.

Once you see the paradigm, you can rewrite it. Once you rewrite it, you can rise above it.

Uncovering Your Money Story

Take a moment to think about these questions honestly. There are no right or wrong answers. Only the truth of what you've been conditioned to believe.

Your Early Money Imprint

- How were your parents with money?
- What repeated phrases about money do you still hear in your head today?

Your Emotional Relationship with Money

- When you think about money, what emotion shows up first?
- Does the idea of becoming wealthy feel empowering or uncomfortable?

Your Current Pattern

- Do your money habits mirror your parents', or are they a reaction against them?
- What do you believe is the real reason you're not where you want to be financially?

What I Learned About My Own Beliefs

When I finally answered these questions honestly, I discovered something I didn't expect.

I had emotionally linked wealth-building with deprivation. Somewhere along the way, I'd absorbed the belief that saving and investing meant missing out on life. That belief led to bad habits: impulsive spending, paycheck-to-paycheck living, and debt.

That single belief cost me years of progress.

But once I shifted my thinking, once I realized investing wasn't giving something up but buying my future freedom, everything changed. The tightness in my chest when I moved money into investments eventually became satisfaction. Same action, completely different meaning.

You'll probably uncover something similar. Some of your beliefs might surprise you. Some might make you uncomfortable. That's a good sign.

Most of your money mindset wasn't chosen. It was handed to you. Passed down, absorbed, and reinforced. Some of it helped you survive. But survival is not the same as freedom.

Ask yourself: Who taught me this? Are they wealthy? Did this belief help them build wealth? Is it helping me or holding me back?

Your current results are the outcome of those old beliefs. If you want new results, you need new beliefs.

Breaking the Wealth Myth

The most destructive belief I had to confront was the idea that wealth is somehow bad. That wealthy people are selfish, corrupt, or morally compromised.

I didn't even know I carried this belief until I noticed my own resistance. Every time I got close to a breakthrough, something inside me would pump the brakes. It took years to realize what was happening: part of me wanted success while another part felt guilty and saw it as maybe morally wrong.

That clash creates cognitive dissonance. Deep tension when your mind is pulled in two directions at once.

This belief is usually a defense mechanism. If you grew up in an environment where wealth seemed out of reach or dangerous, your mind built walls to protect you. It's easier to believe "rich people are bad" than to take full responsibility for building your own future.

Moralizing wealth protects the ego. But it also guarantees you'll never build it.

When you believe wealth is dirty, you will subconsciously avoid it. Then call it fate.

Here's the truth I had to accept: Money isn't about greed. Money is a tool that lets you serve the people you love at a higher level with more time, peace, presence, options, and stability.

The Two Money Mindsets

I operated from scarcity for years without knowing it. I saw every financial decision as a potential threat. I hoarded instead of deployed. I played defense when I should have been building.

That's the scarcity mindset. It's the opposite of thinking like an owner.

Scarcity is a mindset rooted in fear. It tells you money is finite, security is fragile, and risk should be avoided at all costs. It shows up as the employee who stays in a soul-sucking job for "stability" and the would-be investor who hesitates because "the market might crash."

Abundance isn't positive thinking. It's the belief that the world is abundant and that you are the source of outcomes, not their victim.

The shift starts with asking better questions.

Instead of "I can't afford that," ask "How can I afford that?" Instead of "That's too risky," ask "How can I manage the risk?" Instead of "I don't have enough money," ask "How can I create more money?"

These questions make your mind work to solve the problem instead of accepting your circumstances as permanent.

You Are Your Own Oppressor

It's easy to blame "the system" for where you are financially. And to be fair, the system is stacked. The rules changed. Pensions died. The dollar weakened.

The system can limit your starting position. It cannot dictate your ceiling. Only you can do that.

For me, that showed up as avoidance. I could work hard all day, read books, analyze deals, and feel productive. But I kept delaying the one thing that actually moved the needle: talking to people. Calling brokers. Calling sellers. Putting myself out there.

Not because I didn't know what to do. Because once I made the call, the outcome was on me. I was afraid to fail. Busy work felt productive without the risk of rejection.

When you avoid learning how money works, you choose to stay in the dark. When you let fear make your decisions, you choose your current life over the one you say you want.

From here forward, your financial life comes down to one question: "Am I building my freedom, or reinforcing my cage?"

You don't have to answer that out loud. Your decisions will answer it for you.

The good news: if you are your own oppressor, you can also become your own liberator.

Constructive Discontent: The Spark

There's a moment in every person's financial life where something shifts.

You look at your bank account, your stress, your debt, your schedule, the time you're missing with your family, and something inside you finally says: "I'm done living like this."

That moment is constructive discontent.

Most people feel discontent and run from it. They numb it with entertainment, ignore it, or blame the world. Constructive discontent doesn't run. It builds.

It's the inner tension that tells you: "My life does not match my potential, and I'm no longer willing to tolerate it."

Nothing changes until that tension becomes real. Until the pain of staying the same feels worse than the fear of changing.

If you're reading this book, you've probably already felt that moment. Don't waste it.

CHAPTER 4

Protect Your Mind

You've done the internal work. You've identified the beliefs holding you back. You've seen the difference between scarcity and abundance. You've accepted responsibility for your financial future.

Now comes the resistance.

The moment you start changing, the environment will try to restore equilibrium. Not gently. Not consciously. But relentlessly.

Not because people are evil. Not because they hate you. But because your growth threatens their identity. Your ambition forces them to confront their own inaction. And instead of rising with you, most people will try to pull you back down.

This chapter is about hardening your mind and protecting your vision, so doubt, fear, and other people's limitations don't derail your mission.

If you don't control who influences you, you'll end up living someone else's life instead of building your own.

Results Trump Opinions

Early on, I took financial advice from anyone who offered it. Family, coworkers, people who seemed confident. Then I started looking at their actual results. That changed everything.

You've heard it all before:

- "Get a good job."
- "Save for a rainy day."
- "Buy a house, it's the best investment you can make."
- "Put money in your 401(k) and let compound interest do the work."

But look at the people giving that advice. Are they truly living the way you want to live? Are they wealthy? Are they financially free? Or are they just repeating what they were taught to sound smart, despite it not really working for them?

If you wanted to get in shape, you wouldn't take advice from someone who's out of shape. Yet when it comes to money, most people take advice from friends, family, and coworkers stuck in the same paycheck-to-paycheck trap they're trying to escape.

With money, it's hard to tell who's actually winning. Anyone can look successful for a while. New car. Nice vacations. Big house. But you don't see the credit cards, the car loans, the second mortgage, the sleepless nights.

Looking rich and being rich are two very different things.

This isn't about arrogance. It's about aligning your inputs with the outcomes you want.

What About Financial Planners?

Most people don't realize this: a large part of the financial industry is not required to act as a fiduciary at all times. In many settings, the legal standard is "suitability," meaning an advisor can recommend what pays them more, as long as it's considered acceptable for you.

Some advisors switch hats, acting as fiduciaries in one moment and product salespeople the next. The client is rarely told which role is being played.

In Special Forces intel, we never ask, "Does this person sound confident?" We ask, "What are they incentivized to say?"

If the incentive is misaligned, the intel is contaminated. Incentives shape outcomes. Always.

This isn't to call into question their character. Their compensation is tied to assets under management, commissions, or product placement. Cash-flowing businesses, real estate, and ownership strategies don't fit that model, so they're rarely recommended.

Most planners are trained and incentivized to keep you on the traditional path: save, max out the 401(k), open an IRA, invest for decades, and retire later. Not because it's best for you, but because it's how the system pays them.

Take Dave Ramsey. His system teaches people how not to lose. That's valuable if you're drowning in debt. But it doesn't teach you how to win. It keeps you playing defense forever.

Before you accept advice from anyone, ask: "Are they living the life I want, or are they selling the plan I'm trying to escape?"

How do you know for sure? Ask what they own, what cash flow they have, and what they're building. If they can't answer, you already have your answer.

The Crab Bucket

Put one crab in a bucket, and it might escape. Add more crabs, and the others will pull it back down.

People are the same way.

When you start reaching for financial freedom, ownership, or wealth, don't be surprised when others try to drag you back to their level.

Sometimes it's disguised as concern:

- "That's too risky."

- "You should be careful."
- "Are you sure that's a good idea?"

Sometimes it's masked as sarcasm:

- "Must be nice..."
- "Oh, you're doing that entrepreneur thing now?"

I remember telling a friend about my plan to buy my first rental property. His response: "That sounds risky. What if the tenants trash the place?"

He meant well. He was trying to protect me. But he'd never owned a rental, never analyzed a deal, never talked to an investor. He was protecting me from something he didn't understand.

That conversation taught me to be careful about who I shared my plans with.

Your ambition threatens their identity by exposing their inaction. And that makes them uncomfortable.

You are not the problem. Your ambition is not the problem. The problem is they stopped growing, and your growth reminds them of that.

Three Reasons People Doubt You

1. They've seen too many people who never followed through.

Everyone knows someone who talks big but never acts. They assume you're the same. Their past isn't your future.

2. Your success forces them to face themselves.

If you win, it means they could have made different choices. It means they settled. So they downplay what you're doing to protect their own ego. They hope you fail to legitimize their own inaction.

I've watched this happen in real time. When I left my job, some people celebrated with me. Others got quiet. A few made comments that weren't quite jokes. Their discomfort wasn't about me. It was about what my decision revealed about their own choices.

3. They value safety over freedom.

The people closest to you will often resist your growth the most. Not because they don't love you, but because they're scared for you. Their version of "safety" is survival, but survival is not freedom.

In my old job, we called it signal versus noise. Most people are noise. Loud opinions with zero results.

If you keep letting noise into your head, you will keep getting noise in your life.

How to Handle the Noise

Don't argue. Keep moving forward. Most people will never understand your vision until you succeed. They won't believe it until they see it.

Stop explaining and start doing.

Stop sharing your vision with small thinkers. If someone constantly dismisses your ideas, stop giving them updates. They haven't earned a seat at your strategy table.

Upgrade your environment. Your environment quietly sets your upper limit unless you consciously outgrow it. Surround yourself with people who think bigger. Join a mastermind. Go to meetups. Follow builders, not critics.

Train your mind to ignore the noise. The most successful people in the world were all told, "That'll never work." They ignored it. You must, too.

Fear of Failure is Really Fear of Judgment

Most people don't fear failure. They fear looking like a failure in front of people who aren't doing anything with their own lives.

We're not afraid of failing. We're afraid of judgment.

When feeling doubt, reframe it:

- Instead of "What if it doesn't work?" ask: "What if it does?"
- Instead of "I can't afford to fail," say: "I can't afford to stay stuck."

Once you stop letting other people's fear shape your decisions, you can focus on what actually matters: building the life you want instead of defending the life you have.

Once you silence the noise, the only voice left is your own. And now you're accountable for where it's leading you.

That's what comes next.

CHAPTER 5

Define Your Target

Freedom without a target is just boredom with money.

You've hardened your mind and steeled your resolve. You've learned to filter the noise. Now you need to aim at something.

Most people never do this. They stay vague. They say things like, "I want to be rich" or "I want to retire comfortably." But that's not a vision. That's a wish dressed up as a plan.

I was the same way for years. I knew I wanted "more" – more money, more time, more options. But I couldn't describe what that actually looked like. So I drifted. I chased opportunities that didn't align with anything. I made progress in random directions and wondered why I felt stuck.

Everything changed when I got specific.

Why Clarity Matters

When I finally sat down and defined exactly what I wanted, not vague goals, but specific outcomes, decision-making became simple. Opportunities that didn't fit the vision were easy to decline. Distractions lost their pull. Every move became intentional.

Without a target, every opportunity looks like progress. That's how ambitious people waste decades.

If you don't define your target, you will spend your life advancing someone else's mission. Your boss. Your family. Society. They'll fill the vacuum with their priorities, and you'll wake up ten years from now living a life optimized for everyone else's priorities but your own.

Clarity isn't optional. It's the foundation.

Three Ways to Define What You Want

1. The Three-Goal Method

Forget limitations. If failure weren't possible, what would you go after?

Write down three massive goals: things that seem far beyond your current reach. Don't filter for "realistic." Just write.

Here's what I wrote eight years ago:

- Get my pilot's license and own a plane
- Start a foundation that helps veterans build businesses
- Take at least one international vacation every year with my family and another with just my wife

Today, flight school and plane are still on the list. This book is the first brick in that veteran foundation. My wife and I take an international trip every year and took our daughters to Paris last year.

I didn't know how any of it would happen when I wrote those goals. I just knew what I was aiming at. That was enough to start.

2. The Legacy Method

Fast forward to the end of your life. What do you want to be remembered for?

1. What impact do you want to leave behind?
2. What do you want your family to say about you?
3. What will you have built?

Here's what I wrote:

- From my daughters: "He left behind financial freedom and the knowledge so we would never be ruled by money."
- From others: "He helped change the lives of thousands of families by teaching them to be financially free."

When I wrote those statements, they felt impossibly far away. Now they guide every major decision I make.

3. The $10 Million Question

If you inherited $10 million tomorrow, what would you change?

This question strips away the financial excuses and reveals what you actually want. The answer tells you what you're really chasing.

Here's one of mine: Stop rushing off to work. Start spending slow mornings with my wife and kids over a cup of coffee. Put simply, I wanted time. Not money for money's sake. Time.

When I realized that, everything clicked. The goal wasn't wealth accumulation. The goal was buying back my mornings, buying less stress. That specificity changed how I built.

Notice what your $10M answers have in common: none of them are about more stuff. They're about control of time. That tells you exactly what outcome your wealth machine must be built to produce.

Kill "Realistic" Thinking

"Be realistic" is one of the most dangerous phrases you'll ever hear. It sounds practical. It's actually a ceiling disguised as wisdom. "Be realistic" is how average people defend staying average.

The most successful people in the world were not being realistic when they started. They didn't shrink their vision to fit their current circumstances or accept others' view of what's possible. They continued expanding their skills and capabilities to match their vision.

Stop asking if your goals are realistic. Start asking how you can make them real.

Your Mission Brief

Take fifteen minutes. Write this down:

1. Your ideal day. Describe what a perfect Tuesday looks like in your future life. Where are you? Who are you with? What are you doing? What are you not doing?
2. Three ambitious goals. Things that feel just out of reach. Don't filter.
3. Your legacy statement. What do you want to be remembered for? Write it in the voice of someone who knew you.
4. The $10 million test. List two things you would stop doing immediately and two things you would start.

If you don't write it down, it stays a vague idea floating in your head. When you put it on paper, it becomes a target. Targets can be hit.

The Only Person Coming to Save You

No one will hand you the life you want. You either build it or spend your years building someone else's.

You now know two things: who not to listen to, and what you're aiming at.

That's more clarity than most people ever achieve. But clarity without action is just daydreaming.

Vision without structure is fantasy. Next, we build the structure to understand how to buy your freedom.

PART 3

Frameworks for Financial Freedom

CHAPTER 6

The Five Stages of Income

Julian and Ryan were close friends. Two hardworking fathers doing everything they were told was "responsible." And two guys quietly carrying the same question: Why does it feel like the harder I work, the further away freedom gets?

Julian started in hourly work, grinding 12-hour shifts as a security guard. Nights. Weekends. Rotating schedules. He took pride in providing for his family, but every missed bedtime landed like a stone in his chest.

The cruel irony was impossible to ignore: The more he worked to provide for them, the less he actually saw them.

Eventually, he broke into a white-collar logistics role. A salary. Benefits. A title that sounded good. The money was better and his hours were more flexible. But now his time wasn't his own in a different way. Forty hours sometimes meant fifty. Fifty hours meant availability. Availability meant he didn't really own his life.

Julian made low six figures. Other people thought he was "set." But Julian knew better. It was just a nicer-looking cage.

Ryan was trapped in his own version of that same dilemma. He was a highly skilled HVAC technician, one of the best at his company. He loved the work. But like most techs, he was paid by the hour, which meant his income had a ceiling.

Every extra dollar came with a cost: More emergency calls. More missed dinners. More moments with his kids he could never get back.

One night after his third emergency call in a week, Ryan said something that shifted something inside him: "I'm already doing everything the owner does, if not more. Except I don't get paid like the owner does."

Julian and Ryan had different jobs. Different industries. Same frustration. Same late-night conversations: "I thought making more would fix this..." "How are we supposed to retire?" "Why does it feel like I'm working harder but owning less of my own life?"

Two men. Two families. Two different paths leading nowhere close to freedom.

Maybe this sounds like your life too. Maybe you're working harder than ever, trying to be the rock for your family, trying to build a future, yet somehow it still feels like you're sprinting in place.

That quiet frustration isn't because you're doing anything wrong. It's because you're earning the wrong kind of income.

Julian and Ryan weren't broken. The model they were following was.

Two Paths Out

Then Julian discovered real estate.

He came across the idea of house hacking: living in one side of a duplex and renting out the other. His housing cost dropped by more than half. For the first time in his life, he felt money coming in without clocking in.

Julian shared the idea with Ryan. Ryan listened. He found it interesting. But something inside him said: That's not my path.

Julian didn't push. He just kept climbing. Over the next six years, he bought one deal at a time—slow, boring, and relentless. Another duplex that cash-flowed $800 a month. Then a fourplex. Then a 10-unit building and a storage facility. He hired a property manager. He built systems. He stopped trading hours for money.

Eventually, Julian's real estate income passed his salary.

Ryan celebrated every one of Julian's wins. But real estate didn't pull him the same way. He loved HVAC. He understood the business inside and out: the customers, the work, the margins. Real estate was Julian's world. HVAC was his.

He just hated that his income was directly tied to his time.

The sentence "I don't get paid like the owner does" just kept echoing. Ryan didn't need a new industry. He needed ownership.

So Ryan did something hardly anyone thinks to do: He started calling small HVAC companies to see if any owners wanted to retire.

He called for months. Eventually, he found one. A small two-truck operation with a loyal customer base and an owner ready to cash out. Ryan bought it for $200,000 with seller financing and a $30,000 down payment he'd saved over four years.

He kept the one tech. Worked another van himself. Hired another tech. Set up simple systems. Introduced maintenance plans. He didn't get rich on emergency calls. He got rich on recurring revenue and systems.

Within two years his income doubled. Within a few more years, he grew the business to ten vans generating around $3.2 million in revenue with roughly $350,000 in profit.

He made that money while overseeing operations, not turning wrenches. His time was his.

Different path from Julian. Different industry. Same climb. Same destination.

Neither Julian nor Ryan quit their jobs to build this. They didn't work an extra 40 hours a week. Most weeks it was five to ten hours. Sometimes less. Getting up 30 minutes early to read. Listening to podcasts on the commute instead of music. Making calls over lunch. Sending emails in the margins.

Some weeks got heavier, especially around the first deal. Then it slowed back down. That's the rhythm. Consistent effort in the cracks of a normal life. Not a second job. Not a total life overhaul. Just focused hours pointed in the right direction.

And both of their families felt it. More time. Less stress. A future they actually controlled.

The Breakthrough

One night, comparing notes about their journeys, Julian said, "It's wild, man. We did completely different things. But we ended up in the same place."

Ryan nodded. "It wasn't about real estate or HVAC. It was about the type of income. Once we broke free from trading time for money, everything changed."

That was it.

What separated them from most people around them wasn't intelligence, work ethic, or ambition. It was the type of income they were building.

When I first understood this pattern, it explained everything I'd been seeing for years. Why some people escape the W-2 treadmill while others grind for decades with nothing to show. Why Julian's real estate and Ryan's HVAC business both led to the same destination. Why most people stay trapped forever.

This framework is the map I wish someone had given me earlier.

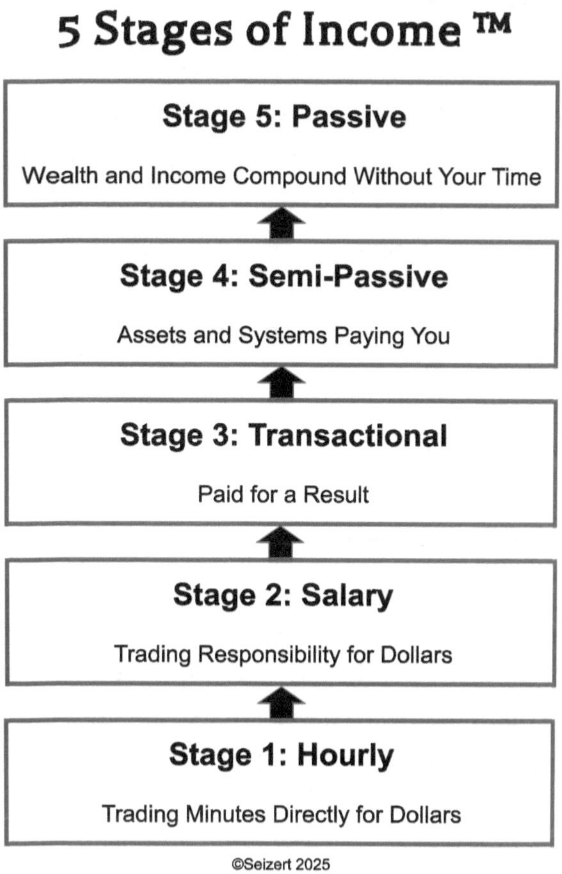

The Five Stages of Income

Stage 1: Hourly — Trading Minutes for Dollars

Nearly everyone starts here. If you aren't working, you aren't earning. Your time is your paycheck.

Wages, overtime, side hustles. Different labels, same cage. You sell your time. Your hours are the product. Your life is the price.

Great place to start. Terrible place to stay.

Stage 2: Salary — Trading Responsibility for Dollars

Now you're paid for the role, not the minutes. It feels better. It looks stable. But it's just a more polished version of the same trap.

Salaried workers feel secure, yet they're capped, controlled, and often working 50-60 hours anyway. Stage 2 is comfort disguised as progress. You think you've advanced, but you're still trading time for money.

Stage 3: Transactional — Paid for Results, Not Hours

The first major jump. Sales. Commissions. Contracting. Performance-based compensation.

Your income becomes tied to your value and output, not your time. The ceiling rises dramatically, but so does volatility. At times it's feast or famine.

Most people never make it here because it requires stepping away from the security of the predictable W-2. And without leverage, Stage 3 can burn you out. There's no coasting. If income stops the moment you stop showing up, you're not in Stage 4 yet.

Stage 4: Semi-Passive — Leverage Through Assets and Systems

Your life changes here. You finally break the time-for-money equation.

You own assets and systems that get paid even when you're not present. Real estate. Equity in businesses. Digital assets. Teams and infrastructure that work whether you clock in or not.

Let me be honest about what semi-passive actually means. Most books sell a fantasy. Sit on a beach while money hits your account. That's not real. Stage 4 takes work to build and still takes some work to maintain. The difference is the math changes. Five or ten hours a week can produce the income equivalent of a full-time job in Stages 1 and 2. With unlimited upside.

Freedom doesn't start at 65. Freedom starts the moment your assets pay for your lifestyle.

This is where Julian landed with his real estate. This is where Ryan landed with his HVAC business. Stage 4 is the version of you your kids will remember. This is where you stop being consumed by work and start being shaped by choice.

This entire book is designed to pull you into Stage 4.

It's the hardest leap you'll make because it's the only one that breaks your dependence. Stages 1 through 3 are all variations of trading time for money. Stage 4 is ownership. Once you're here, Stage 5 isn't a new mountain. It's the same game with less of you required.

Stage 5: Passive — Wealth That Compounds Without You

This is the endgame. Stage 4 gives you freedom from trading time for money. Stage 5 gives you freedom from needing to work at all.

Your money works harder than you ever could:

- Equity that produces distributions
- Assets that appreciate and compound without involvement
- Real estate stabilized and run by teams
- Businesses with leadership in place
- Dividends from long-term holdings
- Royalties from intellectual property

Stage 5 is where the game flips permanently. Your lifestyle is funded by capital, not labor. Someone else is running it all.

Generational wealth. The kind your children inherit not just as money, but as a model.

Once you reach Stage 5, you don't worry about retirement. You think about impact, legacy, and what kind of ancestor you want to be.

One important note: these stages aren't a rigid ladder. You can occupy multiple stages at once. A salaried employee with a rental property is earning Stage 2 and Stage 4 income simultaneously. A business owner might have Stage 3 revenue from client work and Stage 4 income from assets the business owns. You can skip stages entirely, and you can move backward. The stages describe how your income behaves, not a sequence you're required to follow.

The Decision Point

Once you understand the stages, something inside changes.

Before this, most people live in Stage 2 without questioning it. A salary feels stable. Raises feel like progress. There's no obvious reason to doubt the system.

But once you see how income actually works, Stage 2 stops being a destination. It becomes a phase you pass through, not something you build your life on. Use your Stage 1 or 2 income as the foundation to build from as you build Stage 4 income.

The real danger of Stage 2 isn't failure. It's comfort. Comfort delays action. Comfort convinces you there's time. But time is the one thing you don't control.

From here, there are only two paths.

One path runs through the Accumulation Trap. Saving, waiting, hoping the math works out in 30 or 40 years. Using income to build a bigger pile and trusting that someday it will be enough.

The other path runs through ownership. Using income to acquire assets that produce more income, buy back your time, and reduce your dependence on any single system.

Worker and Owner aren't binary categories. They're opposite ends of a spectrum. A W-2 employee who buys a rental property on the side is shifting from one to the other. A business owner who still trades all their time for revenue hasn't fully crossed over yet.

The goal isn't purity. It's direction. The further you move toward ownership, the more control you have and the faster freedom becomes possible. The longer you stay on the Worker side, the harder it is to cross over. Not because you can't. Because nothing in that system teaches you how.

Julian and Ryan didn't just change what they invested in. They changed what they were building toward.

They stopped thinking like Workers. They started thinking like Owners.

Which one are you becoming? And here's the question that will tell you: Are you saving like a Worker, or building like an Owner?

Find Your Freedom Number

Before you move on, you need a target: your Freedom Number.

How much income would you need from Stages 4 and 5 to replace your job?

That's it. If you make $60,000 a year, your first objective is to build $60,000 of asset-based income. Not at age 65. Not someday. While you're still earning your W-2.

When you build Stage 4 income alongside your job, something powerful happens. You're not desperate. You're not gambling. You can reinvest instead of survive. You can take smart risks instead of cling to job security.

The moment your assets pay what your job pays, you're free. Your employer no longer owns your time. You can choose to work or not. You don't have to ask permission for a vacation. You don't have to tolerate toxic bosses or unpredictable schedules.

Hitting your Freedom Number isn't the finish line. It's the starting line.

Once your time is yours again, you have the bandwidth to scale. You can grow your asset base, double your income, triple it. You're not building wealth in the margins of a 40-hour week. You're building it with full focus and full control.

That's why Julian's life changed when his real estate income matched his salary. That's why Ryan exploded his income once he stepped out of the van and into ownership. They replaced their income first. Then they scaled.

Your Freedom Number is just your current income, replaced by assets. Hit that number, and your entire life opens up.

Now It's Your Turn

Julian climbed through real estate. Ryan climbed through HVAC. Different industries. Same stages. Same transition from time-bound income to ownership-based income.

Now it's your turn.

Up to this point, you've been seeing what changed for them. What you haven't seen yet is the structure underneath those changes.

That structure is what the next chapters give you.

First, you'll learn to classify every dollar you own and every dollar you earn using a simple framework: which ones buy freedom, and which ones only look productive. That's the Freedom Matrix.

Then you'll learn why some assets quietly compound and others stall, even when the owner is working hard. That's the Four Drivers of Appreciation.

Then you'll see why these frameworks compress decades into years, and what happens when someone finally connects the pieces.

Finally, you'll map your own financial position the way an operator maps terrain before a mission. Not with vague net worth numbers, but with a Personal Financial Statement that shows you exactly where you are, what's working, what's leaking, and what moves the needle toward Stage 4.

The Five Stages showed you the destination.

Turn the page.

CHAPTER 7

The Freedom Matrix

Most people don't fail financially because they don't work hard. They fail because they spend 40 years building in the wrong quadrant and mistake motion for progress.

Build in the wrong quadrant and your money works against you instead of for you.

The difference between an asset and a liability and how each one actually behaves is the single most important concept in financial literacy.

It sounds simple. Almost everyone gets it wrong.

This chapter gives you the tool to see it. The Freedom Matrix doesn't just classify assets; it diagnoses your financial life in under a minute. It shows you whether you're building freedom or maintaining dependence. And it answers a question most people spend decades avoiding: Am I saving like a Worker, or building like an Owner?

The Definitions That Fail You

According to traditional accounting, anything you own that has value is an asset. By that logic, your house, your car, your furniture, even your boat are all "assets."

In accounting terms, that's technically true. But that definition creates confusion and fails ordinary people in real life.

Does your personal residence send you a check each month? Does your car increase in value the more you drive it? Can you retire on your furniture?

Of course not. Most of those things cost you money every month through payments, maintenance, insurance, and taxes. You're not building wealth. You're quietly draining it.

People get trapped here. If anything with resale value counts as an asset, then buying expensive things feels like investing. It feels like progress. But every month, your "assets" take cash out of your pocket while you work harder just to keep up.

That traditional definition was built for accountants, not for people trying to buy their freedom.

Robert Kiyosaki cracked the door open with a better definition: *An asset puts money in your pocket. A liability takes money out.*

Simple. Clear. And a massive step forward. That sentence woke up millions of people to the trap they were in.

But it's incomplete.

By Kiyosaki's definition, anything that doesn't put money in your pocket today would be labeled a liability. So where does that leave a 401(k), IRA, or even a savings account? Are they neither?

A retirement account isn't a liability. But it's not an asset that creates financial freedom either. Functionally, it's a savings vehicle.

A savings vehicle is a container you feed money into and hope grows over time. It stores value. It does not produce value. It doesn't pay you. It doesn't replace your income. It depends on your continued contributions and decades of patience.

A Freedom Asset is different. It produces income. It appreciates. It can be improved and controlled. It works for you while you sleep.

That distinction matters. If your "asset" only grows when you keep working, and only pays you decades from now, it isn't buying your freedom. It's postponing it.

But most advice misses this entirely.

Everything I read about personal finance fell into one of two camps: cash flow or appreciation. Short-term income or long-term growth.

Traditional advisors preach appreciation. Keep working. Wait forty years. Let compound interest do the work.

Even in real estate, the camps split the same way. Flippers and speculators chase appreciation. Buy, hope it goes up, sell. Cash flow purists ignore equity entirely. If it doesn't pay you monthly, they don't care what it's worth.

Business acquisition circles do the same thing. Some buy for cash flow. Others buy to flip.

Pick your lane. That was the message.

But what I was reading didn't match reality.

When I studied what truly wealthy, financially free people were actually doing, the ones who had real freedom, not just high incomes, I found something different. They weren't choosing one or the other. They bought, built, or created assets that did both.

That was the missing link. Cash flow creates freedom. Income you don't have to directly work for. Equity growth creates wealth. Net worth that snowballs into more cash flow over time. The people who escaped weren't optimizing for one. They were stacking both.

And when you look at what happens when people only chase one, the trap becomes obvious.

If you only chase appreciation, you build wealth on paper but no freedom. Your net worth grows, but you still need your paycheck. You can't touch the gains without selling. You're rich on a spreadsheet and stuck in real life.

If you only chase cash flow, you build income but no scale. You've replaced your paycheck, but there's no equity to create growth or leverage into the next deal. No way to snowball. You've escaped the job, but you've hit a ceiling.

The people who actually get free do both. Cash flow funds the life. Appreciation builds the ladder to climb higher.

But there's a third element that separates Freedom Assets from everything else: control.

When you control the asset, you can apply your knowledge and skill to increase cash flow, which increases value, which builds more equity to redeploy. You're not waiting on the market. You're not hoping. You're driving the outcome. That's what creates speed. That's how people compress decades into years.

To actually buy your freedom, you need a model that accounts for both appreciation and cash flow. That's what the Freedom Matrix does.

Now let's name what you just found.

The Freedom Matrix

The Five Stages showed you the structure of your income and what level of freedom it can buy. The Freedom Matrix shows you where your money lives, where your effort goes, and whether both are moving you toward Stage 4 or keeping you stuck. Remember the first two questions:

1. Does it produce income?
2. Does it go up in value over time or down?

The answers create four possible combinations. Those four combinations become the four quadrants of the Freedom Matrix.

The vertical axis measures appreciation. Does it go up in value or down? The horizontal axis measures income. Does it pay you or cost you?

Where your money sits on this grid determines whether it's building your freedom or working against you.

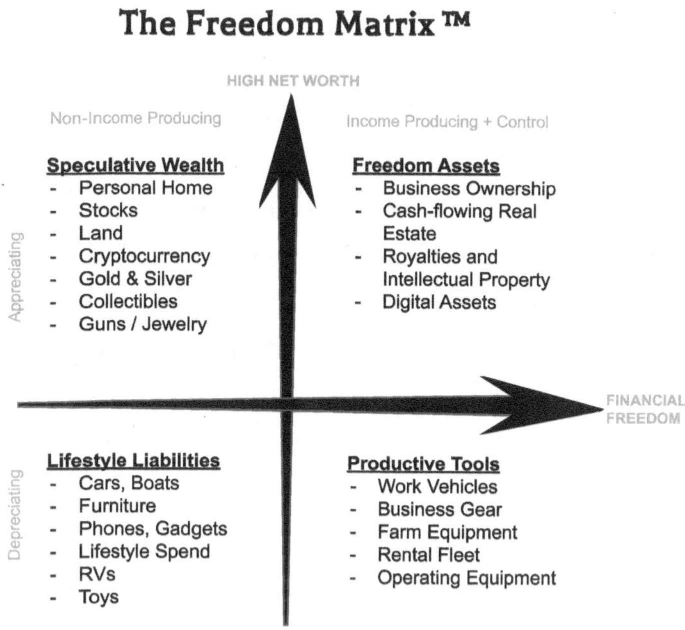

The Freedom Matrix: Only the top-right quadrant builds both net worth and income you control. Everything else either keeps you stuck or slows you down.

Bottom Left: Lifestyle Liabilities

The middle class gets crushed here.

This is where money goes to die quietly. Every dollar here is a dollar that will never work for you, never come back, and never buy you a single hour of freedom. You don't have a spending problem. You have a direction problem. And this quadrant is the wrong direction.

These items cost money every month and lose value every year. Cars. Boats. Furniture. Electronics. Lifestyle creep.

Everyone around you normalizes this quadrant. Society applauds it. Marketers fuel it. But nothing in this box brings you closer to freedom. It does the exact opposite.

The issue isn't whether you have Lifestyle Liabilities. Everyone does. Even wealthy people in Stage 4 and 5. A car is a liability, but mostly necessary.

The issue is whether you let them control you.

Most people build their entire sense of success on the appearances in this quadrant. After saving a little for retirement, they spend most of their money here because that's what everyone around them models. They buy a nice car because it makes them look and feel successful.

The wealthy don't avoid Lifestyle Liabilities. They just let their assets pay for them not their labor.

Control how much you spend here until you're free.

Top Left: Speculative Wealth

This is the quadrant the system built for Workers. It keeps you working, keeps you waiting, and ensures you benefit last from your own effort and your own money.

I lived here for years. If you're here, you're doing exactly what you were told: saving into retirement accounts, buying index funds, watching the balance climb on a screen you can't touch for decades. You feel responsible. You feel like you're "on track." But track to where? You're building a pile you can't use, hoping the math works out before your body or your patience gives out. This isn't investing. It's waiting. And waiting has never bought anyone their freedom.

These things may appreciate over time and increase your net worth on paper, but they don't send you a check each month. You keep shoveling money in for decades hoping for a better return than a savings account. The Accumulation Trap in its purest form.

Over long enough timelines, many of these assets will likely go up. That's exactly why they feel safe.

But appreciation without income and control doesn't create freedom. You're guessing on markets you can't influence, timelines you don't control, and outcomes you can't accelerate. Your only lever is waiting. And while you wait, you still need a paycheck.

The problem isn't that these assets don't work. The problem is that they only work if you keep working.

Stocks. Index funds. Crypto. Retirement accounts. Growth assets with no cash flow.

There's nothing inherently wrong with these. I call them "speculative" because you can't depend on them to buy your freedom. They rise and fall with markets you can't influence, provide zero income, and leave the outcome to timing and luck.

If you invest $1,000 and hit a 10x winner, you have $10,000. Exciting, but it doesn't change your life. Hit another 10x, you're at $100,000. Still not freedom. You can't live on it long, and it won't replace your job.

Speculation only becomes life-changing when the starting pile is already massive, or when lightning strikes multiple times. That's not a strategy. That's hope.

Sure, hope can be part of a portfolio, but it can't be the foundation of your freedom.

The "if only" stories live here. If you had bought Bitcoin in 2015. If you had bought Nvidia before the boom. Of course those would have paid off...in hindsight. But they were gambles at the time.

There's nothing wrong with putting some money here. Just be honest about what it is: a bet, not a freedom strategy.

Bottom Right: Productive Tools

This quadrant is the toolbox, not a business. Nothing here makes you free by itself. But everything here can make freedom faster, if it's attached to an ownership structure on the right side of the matrix.

These items support income or business activity, but they depreciate over time. A work vehicle. A camera kit. Farm equipment. Software systems. Tools of the trade. A tool without a system is just an expense.

A tool inside an ownership structure is a force multiplier. The question isn't whether you spend here. It's whether what you're building justifies the spend.

They're important. They enable your income machines. But they don't set you free by themselves. They're tools, not wealth engines.

A tool only becomes powerful when it's attached to a system you control. On its own, it improves efficiency, but efficiency without ownership just makes you a better worker.

This is where Stage 3 and 4 earners put money to support their businesses. Necessary, but not the goal.

Top Right: Freedom Assets™

This is where Owners build. People who bought or built something that produces income, appreciates in value, and responds to their effort. Not just ownership on paper. Real control. You drive the results. You improve the asset. You decide what happens next.

Only one quadrant builds freedom by design, not by luck. If you're here, your money works on your schedule. Your net worth and your cash flow grow together. You're not watching a screen and hoping. You're operating, improving, and compounding. This is the only quadrant where the timeline is in your hands.

And this is the only quadrant where the end result isn't just wealth. It's agency. The ability to say no. The ability to walk away. The ability to be present for the things that actually matter.

These assets share four characteristics:

1. *They produce cash flow.* Income arrives whether you work or not.
2. *They appreciate over time.* Your net worth grows alongside your income.
3. *They can be controlled and improved.* You influence the outcome directly.
4. *They can be repeated and scaled.* Success isn't a one-time event.

That third characteristic is the killer distinction. Control means you can improve the asset. You benefit most from the value you create. That's what creates speed.

With Speculative Wealth, you're betting on markets you don't control, assets you can't influence, and income you can't engineer. You're a passenger.

With Freedom Assets, you're the mastermind and operator. You can raise rents. You can improve margins. You can add revenue streams. You can fix problems. You can force appreciation by decision, not by waiting.

That's why timelines collapse in this quadrant. Control compresses time.

Real estate that cash flows. Businesses with recurring revenue. Digital assets that produce income. Equity in companies you control.

Only here can you create outsized results without needing outsized capital. You don't need to be early and lucky. You need structure, leverage, and ownership.

Freedom Assets grow your income and your net worth at the same time.

The self-made wealthy focus on becoming Owners in this quadrant relentlessly. It pays their bills, replaces their salaries, grows their income, and buys back their time.

Stage 4 and Stage 5 are built here. Buy and build in this quadrant, and the timeline most people accept as "normal" collapses from decades to years.

What takes most people a lifetime in Speculative Wealth can be accomplished in a few focused years with Freedom Assets.

Freedom is actually bought and built here.

Now look at your own life through this lens. Ask yourself three questions about anything you own or pay into:

1. Does it produce income?
2. Does it go up or down in value over time?

3. Do you have any control over either of those?

To show you what I mean, pick three things. Your car. Your house. Your 401(k). A rental property. Whatever comes to mind. Ask yourself those three questions about each one. Be honest.

If you're like most people, you just realized something uncomfortable: almost everything you own lives on the left side of this matrix. Your car, bottom left. Your retirement accounts, top left. Your house, top left at best. Your furniture, your phone, your lifestyle, bottom left.

The things you were told were assets are quietly working against you.

I had a growing 401(k) balance and felt like I was "doing the right thing." But the number on the statement went up, and my freedom didn't. And it wouldn't for another thirty plus years if I stayed on that path.

When I first mapped my own finances using this framework, I didn't like what I saw. Most of what I owned lived on the left side of the matrix. I'd been a Worker for years, building in the wrong quadrant and bleeding from another, without realizing it.

The moment I understood the difference between storing value and producing value, everything shifted. You're not broke. You're not lazy. You're not failing. You're following the default program, the one every financial advisor, HR department, and well-meaning parent handed you. And the default program doesn't end in freedom. It ends in "hopefully enough."

The Freedom Matrix doesn't judge you for being here. It shows you where "here" actually is, so you can decide whether to stay.

The Big Insight

Most people spend their entire lives on the left side of the matrix. They work, save, and invest, yet remain dependent on their paycheck because their money lives in places that consume cash, not create it.

The financially free live on the right side. Their net worth and their income grow at the same time.

The Freedom Matrix shows you where your money lives today. The Five Stages show you where your income comes from. Together, they reveal your current position and your likely trajectory.

They also become a decision filter. Every opportunity, every investment, every career move can now be run through one question: Is this building the left side of my matrix, or the right?

Workers sell their time to earn income so they can spend in the bottom left and save in the top left, hoping it all works out decades from now. Their time feeds consumption and speculation. They work to fund a retirement plan that might turn into income someday. That's the default loop, and it never breaks on its own.

Owners use their hours to buy, build, and grow assets in the top right. They use the bottom right to support those assets. Tools, systems, and infrastructure powering their income machines. Their time compounds into ownership, income, and control. The money circulates. Income funds acquisition. Acquisition builds equity. Equity unlocks more acquisition. The loop compounds.

This is where the Five Stages and the Freedom Matrix lock together. Your Stage tells you how you earn. Your quadrant tells you where it goes. A Worker earns at Stage 2, spends in the bottom left, and saves in the top left. An Owner earns at Stage 4 or builds toward it, deploys capital into the top right, and uses the bottom right to support those assets.

Same starting point. Same 24 hours. But the Worker's loop drains and traps. The Owner's loop builds and frees. And the only difference is which quadrant gets fed.

The Engine of Wealth

The Freedom Matrix shows you where to focus your money, time, and effort, which quadrant actually builds freedom, and which keeps you tied to your job.

But there's another question: Why do assets in the top right work so differently from everything else?

To answer that, you need to understand what actually makes assets grow. The next chapter reveals the four forces behind every asset's value and the one force you can actually command.

Turn the page.

CHAPTER 8

The Four Drivers of Appreciation

Your net worth can climb for 30+ years while your life stays owned by someone else.

I watched this happen to myself for years. My 401(k) balance climbed. My home equity grew. On paper, I was "building wealth." But nothing changed. I still needed my paycheck. I still had no control over my time. I still couldn't walk away.

Then I bought my first rental property. Within 18 months, I'd raised rents, cut expenses, and increased the net operating income by $14,000 a year. The property was suddenly worth $200,000 more than I paid for it. Not because the market moved. Because I made the asset better.

On a deal under a million dollars, one operational cycle produced more wealth than a decade of saving.

That was the moment I understood: not all appreciation is created equal.

Most people think asset growth is something that happens to them. Markets rise, values climb, net worth increases. They watch the numbers and hope.

But there's one type of appreciation you can actually command. One driver that puts you in control. One force that compresses decades into years.

This chapter shows you all four drivers and why only one of them actually buys your freedom.

The Illusion Your Net Worth Creates

Every quadrant in the Freedom Matrix can raise your net worth.

A new car can temporarily increase your net worth on paper. A house adds equity as you pay it down. Stocks and crypto rise with markets. A rental property or business grows as income increases.

Each boosts your net worth, but their real-life effects couldn't be more different.

Net worth is simple: the value of your assets minus liabilities. It tells you what you own after subtracting what you owe.

But net worth alone doesn't tell you:

- Whether you can stop working
- Whether your money is working for you
- How much of your life is funded by assets
- Whether you can buy back your time

A house worth more doesn't pay your bills. A retirement account with a higher balance doesn't cover next month's expenses.

Net worth shows ownership. Cash flow shows freedom.

People chase a number instead of building the income that actually changes their life.

The Four Drivers of Appreciation

Appreciation isn't magic. It's not random. And it doesn't work the same across all quadrants of the Freedom Matrix.

Four forces cause asset values to rise. Only one leads to actual freedom. The others can increase your net worth without changing your life.

Driver 1: Monetary Inflation

The dollar loses value, so everything priced in dollars rises.

The base layer of all appreciation: your house, index funds, gold, Bitcoin. Everything denominated in dollars rises simply because the currency underneath it is weakening.

You can feel richer and still fall behind. If inflation was 4% and your home appreciated 4%, the net effect on your wealth is zero.

Inflation-based appreciation is a mirage. It looks like progress. Nothing in your daily life gets easier.

Driver 2: Supply and Demand Pressure

When more people want something than supply allows, prices rise. Real estate markets, hot stocks, commodities, collectibles–anything where human desire collides with scarcity.

At the macro level, this is outside your control. You don't decide population trends, zoning laws, interest rates, or capital flows.

At the micro level, skilled operators can reposition an asset to better serve existing demand. Flippers, developers, and turnaround specialists improve the product, upgrade the use, or remove bottlenecks. And the market rewards that with a higher price.

But it's still Driver 2. It's transactional because it's exit-dependent. It only pays when you sell. You're riding the wave better than most, but you're still riding the wave.

You can make money here. You just can't build a scalable, controllable freedom machine here.

Driver 3: Investor Sentiment

Sometimes an asset rises not because it produces more income, but because investors are willing to pay more for the same income.

This happens when interest rates drop and borrowing gets cheap, when liquidity floods the system, or when a sector becomes fashionable and money piles in.

The asset didn't improve. The income didn't grow. The machine didn't get better. The market just decided it was worth more.

You see it in real estate when cap rates compress. In stocks when price-to-earnings ratios expand. In crypto when speculation detaches price from any cash flow.

Driver 3 is real and can be powerful. But you didn't cause it. You can't control it. And you can't predict when it reverses.

What the market gives, the market can take.

Driver 3 is a tailwind, not a strategy. If your freedom depends on investors staying excited, you don't have freedom. You have exposure.

Driver 4: Operational Performance

When an asset produces more income, it becomes more valuable.

True for rental properties, private businesses, and publicly traded companies. Higher net income equals higher value. The principle is universal across asset classes. The difference is who's in control.

When a stock rises because the company improves earnings, you benefit, but you had nothing to do with it. You're last in line to receive the benefit. You're a minority owner with no authority, no levers, no ability to change the outcome.

When your rental property or business produces more income because you raised rents, cut costs, added revenue streams, or tightened operations, you caused that. You're first in line to benefit because you created the result.

The mechanism is the same. The control is not.

With stocks, Driver 4 happens for you. With Freedom Assets, Driver 4 happens because of you.

You raise prices strategically. You improve operations. You cut waste. You add revenue streams. You tighten management. You increase efficiency.

The market sets the environment.

Operators control the machine inside it.

Driver 4 builds the engine. Drivers 1, 2, and 3 determine what the engine sells for. Driver 4 doesn't just grow value. It shortens time. It lets you compress decades of waiting into a few operational cycles.

The first form of appreciation that actually changes your life. It produces cash flow today and equity growth tomorrow. That equity can be reinvested, leveraged, or redeployed into more income-producing assets creating a compounding loop of income and value.

The middle class is never taught this loop. Ordinary people build extraordinary wealth this way. This is how freedom stops being a someday goal and becomes an engineered outcome.

Only One Driver Creates Freedom

Inflation can make numbers go up. Scarcity can make prices rise. Investor excitement can make assets look more valuable.

None of those make you free. They all depend on forces outside your control.

Only one driver actually changes your life: Operational Performance. It's the only driver where:

1. You get paid now, not just someday
2. Your asset becomes more valuable because you made it better
3. Your equity grows as a byproduct of cash flow, not speculation and inflation.

And here's what most people never realize: when you increase income, the value goes up. When the value goes up, you have more equity. That equity can be pulled out and used to acquire another asset or expand the current one. That new asset creates more income, which increases value, which creates more equity.

The cycle repeats. Each improvement funds the next move. That's how ordinary people compress decades into years.

Every other driver can make you richer on paper. Driver 4 is the only one that can buy your time back.

Forced Appreciation: Pulling the Lever

You'll hear real estate investors talk about "forcing" appreciation through renovations, repositioning, or operational improvements.

Forced appreciation isn't a separate driver. It's the lever you pull to activate the drivers. It's the act of converting control into value.

When you renovate and sell, you're pulling Driver 2, increasing market desirability and capturing a higher price at exit.

When you renovate and raise rents or improve operations, you're pulling Driver 4, increasing the income, which permanently raises value.

Forced appreciation is one of the most powerful wealth engines on the planet.

Buy a 10-unit apartment building, a roofing company, a 100-unit storage facility, or a car wash. Come in and raise the net income. Cut unnecessary expenses. Increase prices. Improve operations.

If you increase net operating income by $12,000 a year, you haven't just put $12,000 more in your pocket. At a 7% cap rate, you've increased the property's value by over $170,000 without having to wait years for the market to move.

In business, the same principle applies. Increase net cash flow and value rises. The multiple differs, but the mechanism is identical.

That kind of income improvement can often be achieved in months, not decades. And it's repeatable.

Driver 2 forced appreciation compounds by recycling capital. You sell, take the profit, and buy the next deal. The machine changes every time.

Driver 4 forced appreciation compounds by keeping the machine. You increase income, pull equity, and use it to buy more machines. Now you have two. Then three. Each one feeds the next.

One is transactional. The other is systemic. Both build wealth. Only one builds an ever-growing income engine.

The Picture is Complete

Now you have the full picture.

The Freedom Matrix shows you where to focus your money, time, and effort. The Five Stages show you the structure of your income. The Four Drivers show you why assets grow and which part of that growth you can actually command.

You know the difference between riding markets and engineering outcomes. Between hoping for appreciation and forcing it. Between owning assets and operating machines.

But knowing the frameworks isn't enough. The next chapter shows you what happens when someone finally connects the pieces and why the timeline most people accept as "normal" collapses when they do.

Turn the page.

CHAPTER 9

Why Decades Become Years

Alex and I served together. Smart guy. Disciplined. The kind of person who did everything right. Good job, steady promotions, maxed his retirement accounts, bought a house in a nice neighborhood. He has a wife, Haley, and two little boys he loves deeply and talked about constantly. He always said he was working hard to give them everything.

But he was never there because he was working.

We'd grab coffee occasionally when our paths crossed. I'd tell him what I was working on. The rentals, the storage units, the goal to replace my salary with assets. He'd listen, then shrug it off, "That's cool, man. I just don't have time for all that. I'm gonna keep grinding and let the retirement account do its thing."

Fair enough. Different paths. I didn't push.

We lost touch for a few years. Life happens. Then we reconnected at a mutual friend's retirement ceremony. I had walked away from my job at 39. He was still in the same role. Actually, a promotion or two higher. More responsibility. More stress. Longer hours. His boys were in high school now.

This time, the shrug was gone.

"All right, man. I need you to actually explain this to me. How did you get out? What would you do if you were starting now?" He paused. "Is it too late for me?"

That question hit me. Not because the answer was complicated. Because I'd watched him have the information for years and me as a resource, but never act on it.

We grabbed coffee the next morning and had a real conversation this time.

I explained the Five Stages of Income to him like I just did for you. Then I asked where his income came from.

"Salary. And a bonus if the department hits its numbers."

"That it?"

"That's it."

Stage 2. Every dollar required him to show up. He had a good job, but he didn't own anything that paid him without his presence.

"There's nothing wrong with Stage 2," I said. "But it can't buy your freedom. Freedom starts at Stage 4. That's when you own an asset or system that creates income whether you're there or not."

He leaned forward. "Okay. So what are those things? What assets actually do that?"

I grabbed a napkin and sketched the Freedom Matrix like I just did for you. Four quadrants. Two questions: Does it produce income? Does it go up or down in value?

"Stage 4 and 5 income comes from assets in this quadrant," I said, tapping the top right. "Freedom Assets. They produce cash flow. They appreciate over time. And you can control and improve them. That combination is what compresses time."

Then I asked where his money lived right now.

He listed off his 401(k), an IRA, equity in his house, and a truck almost paid off.

I pointed to the napkin. "Your retirement accounts sit here. Top left. Speculative Wealth. They might grow, but they don't pay you. You can't touch them for decades without penalties. You don't control them. You just hope.

"Your house is part appreciation, part liability. It costs you every month. Mortgage, taxes, insurance, repairs. And your truck? Bottom left. Loses value. Costs money. Lifestyle Liability."

He stared at the napkin. "So nothing I own is actually working for me?"

"Not yet. Everything lives on the left side. That's why your net worth keeps climbing but your freedom doesn't. The left side stores wealth. The right side creates it."

He looked up. "You said control compresses time. How does that actually work?"

I walked him through the Four Drivers of Appreciation like I just did for you. Inflation. Supply and demand. Investor sentiment. Operational performance.

"The first three happen to you," I said. "You can't control them. The market moves, your assets go up or down, and you just watch. That's what your 401(k) depends on. That's why it takes decades.

"But Driver 4 is different. Operational performance. When you own a Freedom Asset, you control the income. You can raise rents. Cut expenses. Add revenue streams. Every dollar of increased income makes the asset worth more."

"So you're not waiting for the market," he said. "You're forcing it."

"Exactly. And here's where it compounds." I drew a circle on the napkin. "I call it the Value Loop.

"Every Freedom Asset runs its own loop. You increase income, the value goes up, increasing equity. You pull some of that equity out through a refinance or sale. Not to spend. To buy another asset or bigger asset. Or expand the current one. That new asset starts its own Value Loop. Now you've got two loops running. Then three. Then ten."

I drew more loops on the napkin, each one feeding the next.

"Income increases value. Value creates equity. Equity funds expansion or acquisition. And that creates new income. Each asset is its own loop. And each loop can spin up more loops. That's how ordinary people build extraordinary wealth in years instead of decades. Not by saving harder. By expanding and multiplying machines."

He sat back. "So the same years I spent saving and hoping my retirement accounts would grow, you spent buying things you could improve. And every improvement made the next move easier."

"That's it. Same ten years. Completely different results. I didn't build one thing. I built a system of loops that kept feeding each other."

By the end of that conversation, Alex didn't just understand what to do differently. He understood why the last decade had felt like running in place.

He had worked hard. He had earned well. He had done what he was taught. But every dollar he made went to the left side of the matrix. Every hour he worked bought him a little more net worth on paper but zero freedom in his actual life. He was richer than he was ten years ago. And just as trapped.

The frameworks weren't complicated. They were the explanation for everything he'd been feeling. And the Value Loop was the piece that connected them all.

"So is it too late?" he asked again.

"No," I said. "But the next ten years are going to pass whether you act or not. The question is where you'll be standing when they do."

Warren Buffett put it simply: "If you don't figure out how to make money while you sleep, you'll work until you die."

The difference between us wasn't talent or luck. It was the model. He was playing a linear game. I was building an exponential one.

Linear vs Exponential

When you trade time for money, you're playing a game that can't scale. One hour equals one hour's worth of pay. One month equals one month's salary. Want more income? Ask for a raise, trade more hours, or find a new job. But that's it. That's the model.

There's only so much time in a day. If your income depends on your presence, your income is capped by your calendar.

Let's say you get a raise of $5 more per hour. That feels like progress. But that's $200 more per week. $800 a month. $9,600 per year. Does it change your life? Not really.

Here's what happens: you breathe easier for a few months. Then your lifestyle expands. The bills creep back up. That raise becomes your new baseline. And now you're grinding harder for the same feeling of barely enough.

That's linear growth. Predictable. Slow. Capped. It scales in inches.

Massive effort in a linear system can't produce exponential results. It can't buy your time back. It can't compound. It can't scale. It keeps you stuck in a game where the only way to earn more is to give more of your life away.

Now let me show you exponential.

We own over 3,500 self-storage units. If we raise rent by an average of just $10 per unit, we instantly increase our income by $35,000 per month. $420,000 per year. No extra hours worked. No overtime. Just one decision inside a scalable system.

And because commercial real estate is valued based on income, that same rent increase added roughly $6,000,000 in equity.

This is the same principle that allowed us to scale from one facility to two, then to six, then to eight.

Each asset increased cash flow, which increased borrowing power, which increased deal size and optionality. Each win wasn't consumed. It was redeployed.

That's why this doesn't stop at eight. Ten, twenty, and beyond aren't goals. They're predictable outcomes of the same system running again and again.

Remember Ryan in Chapter 6? Same principle, different asset. When he bought that small HVAC company, it was doing around $400,000 in gross revenue. He introduced maintenance plans, tightened operations, added a second truck, then more trucks. Within a few years, he grew it to $3.2 million in revenue with $350,000 in annual profit and a valuation of around $1.3M. He didn't work more hours. He just built a better machine. And because businesses are valued on earnings, his equity multiplied right alongside his income.

Different asset class. Same Value Loop.

Compare these to the traditional path:

To earn $420,000 at a job, most people would have to climb the ladder for decades or hold a role that consumes their entire life.

To save $6 million? If you invested $2,000 a month at 7%, it would take over 43 years.

I created my numbers with something that took less time than sending an email. Ryan created his by applying Driver 4 to a business instead of a building.

Can I do it again next year? Yes. Can Ryan expand to a second location or add another service line? Absolutely. That's the Value Loop in action. That's exponential.

The wealthy don't grind harder. They don't chase raises. They build machines that pay them whether they show up or not.

You don't escape the rat race by running faster. You escape by building a different machine.

A mentor of mine once told me, "Once I started valuing my time more than my money, everything changed."

At first it sounded like a coffee mug quote. Then he broke it down.

Would you rather have $100 today or a year from now? Easy. Today. That's the time value of money.

Now ask yourself: Would you rather have financial freedom at 40 or at 65?

Same logic. Time is more valuable when you're young. You have energy, health, family, and opportunity. You can actually enjoy freedom.

But most people trade their best years for a shot at maybe retiring in their mid-60s.

My dad did that. Worked his whole life. Retired at 64. One year later, he was gone.

That's when it solidified in my mind that time isn't just more valuable than money. It's the reason we want money in the first place.

The wealthy understand this. They don't ask, "How can I make more money?" They ask, "How can I make money without trading my time?"

They'll invest weeks structuring a deal that pays them for decades. One move, executed well, can create a lifetime of income.

Meanwhile, most people spend 40 hours a week chasing dollars that vanish the moment the bills clear.

Are the things you're doing today moving you toward freedom, or just keeping you busy?

Most people try to earn more and save more by doubling down on the same linear model that trapped them. Second job. Another degree. A promotion. All of it feels responsible. But it's still one-to-one. More time for slightly more money. The return never outruns the hours spent.

Freedom doesn't come from squeezing more hours into your week. It comes from building things that break the link between your labor and your income.

Stop asking, "How can I work more to earn more?"

Start asking, "What can I build once that pays me forever?"

One path owns your time. The other gives it back. The next step is finding out which path your money, effort, and equity are on right now.

CHAPTER 10

The Financial Statement

You just saw how the Value Loop compounds wealth in years instead of decades. But here's the question: Is your money actually in the loop?

Two people can have the same net worth and be living completely different lives.

One is grinding, stressed, dependent on every paycheck. The other is building momentum, watching cash flow in, compounding toward freedom. Same number on paper. Completely different engines underneath.

The first time I mapped my own finances this way, I wanted to look away. I had a growing retirement account, some equity in my home, a decent salary. On paper, I looked like I was winning. But when I traced where every dollar actually went, the truth was brutal: almost everything I owned was draining me. My "assets" were liabilities in disguise. My net worth was rising while my freedom stayed frozen.

That's when I understood: the system trains you to watch balances. Freedom requires you to watch flows. This is why the financial statement is important.

Same Net Worth, Different Futures

Let's look at three people. Each has a net worth of $100,000. Same number. Completely different realities.

Person A: $100,000 in Retirement Accounts

IRA, 401(k), or similar.

Top-left quadrant: Speculative Wealth.

This person did everything right. They maxed out the company match. They invested consistently for years. They watched the balance grow and felt responsible.

But that $100,000 doesn't pay them anything today. They can't touch it for decades without penalties. They have no control over how it's invested or when the market decides to drop 30%. If they lose their job tomorrow, that money can't help them.

No cash flow. No control. Not building freedom. Looks responsible. Stays dependent on their job. Safe, but stuck.

Person B: $100,000 in Home Equity and a Car

$70K in home equity, $30K in a depreciating vehicle. Combination of Speculative Wealth and Lifestyle Liabilities.

This person looks successful. Nice house in a good neighborhood. Reliable car in the driveway. Friends and family assume they're doing well.

But that home equity is locked inside the walls. They can't access it without selling or borrowing. Meanwhile, the mortgage, taxes, insurance, and maintenance drain cash every month. The car looks like an asset on paper, but it loses value every day and costs money to own.

No income. Rising monthly expenses. Equity trapped. Car losing value. Feels wealthy because net worth is climbing. Lifestyle collapses the moment the paycheck stops.

Person C: $100,000 in a Freedom Asset

Equity in a rental property, storage facility, or small business. Top-right quadrant: Freedom Assets.

This person owns something that works for them. Every month, income arrives whether they show up or not. The asset appreciates over time. And if they want to grow faster, they can improve it, raise rents, cut costs, or expand.

Money comes in every month. Value grows over time. Can be improved and controlled. Can be leveraged to acquire more. Their net worth isn't just a number. It's an income machine. It's in the Value Loop.

Same $100K. Only one has freedom.

Net worth can grow in every quadrant of the Freedom Matrix. Cash flow only grows in the top right. That's the difference between looking wealthy and actually buying your time back.

Most people are some combination of A and B. Almost none are building toward C.

The Personal Financial Statement

If cash flow creates freedom, how do you measure it? How do you see what your money and assets are actually doing?

That's where the Personal Financial Statement (PFS) comes in.

The Freedom Matrix shows where your money sits. The Drivers of Appreciation explain why value changes. The PFS shows how cash actually moves through your life each month.

The PFS has two parts:

1. Income Statement – the flow of money in and out
2. Balance Sheet – what you own and what you owe

Together, they answer one question with brutal clarity: Is your money working for you, or are you still working for it?

And once you see the answer, you can never unsee it.

Personal Financial Statement

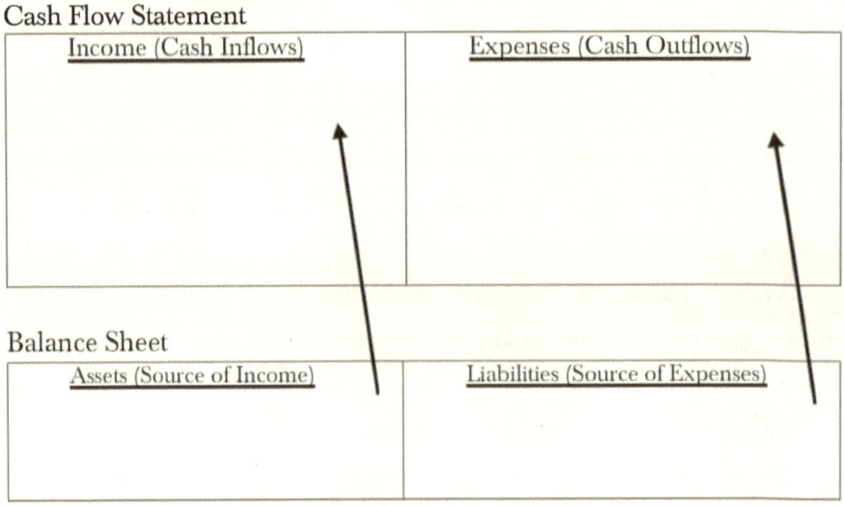

The Direction of Flow

Here's the fundamental insight:

Money must flow from assets to you, not from you to things.

Assets create income. Liabilities create expenses. One side builds wealth. The other drains it.

Most things people think are assets—their primary home, their car, their vacation property—are actually pulling money out every month. They show up on the balance sheet as assets, but functionally, they behave like liabilities.

If it doesn't generate income and you're the one feeding it, it's not building your freedom. It's trapping you.

The fundamental problem is that it's not just about how much you earn. It's not even about how much you save.

The middle-class trap is letting liability growth outpace asset growth while saving money every month into Speculative Investments for their retirement.

This road will never lead to freedom. Let it sink in. When I learned this, it felt like an epiphany.

The Worker vs. The Owner

Two people can earn the same income, but their financial statements tell completely different stories.

The Worker's Approach:

- One income source: a job (Stage 1, 2, or 3)
- Saves into retirement accounts (Speculative Wealth)
- Buys liabilities disguised as assets: big house, new car
- As income rises, lifestyle inflates to match
- Owns zero Freedom Assets

Result: All money flows out. Nothing flows in. Hope to retire at 65.

The Worker's PFS

Cash Flow Statement

Income (Cash Inflows)	Expenses (Cash Outflows)
Salary	*Housing Payment*
	Utilities
	Phone
	Internet
	Taxes
	Credit Card Payment
	Student Loan Payment
	Car Loan Payment
	Car Expenses

Balance Sheet

Assets	Liabilities (Source of Expenses)
401(k)	*Mortgage*
IRA	*Car Loan*
	Credit Card Balance
	HELOC
	Student Loans

Did you notice the direction of cash flow? Every arrow points outward. Their life is a leak.

The Owner's Approach:

- Multiple income streams from cash-flowing assets (Freedom Assets)
- Uses asset income to cover expenses
- As assets grow, so does freedom
- Cash flows inward and compounds

Result: Can stop working whenever asset income exceeds expenses.

The Owner's PFS

Cash Flow Statement

Income (Cash Inflows)	Expenses (Cash Outflows)
Rental Income	*Housing Payment*
Business Income	*Utilities*
K1 Business Distributions	*Phone*
Dividends	*Internet*
Royalties	*Taxes*
Interest Income	*Credit Card Payment*
	Car Expenses

Balance Sheet

Assets (Source of Income)	Liabilities (Source of Expenses)
Rental Real Estate	*Personal Mortgage*
Business Ownership	*Personal Loans*
Dividend Producing Stock/Bond	*Credit Card Balances*
Intellectual Property	
Promissory Note	

The arrows point inward first. Income enters from the balance sheet before it leaves. That's control.

When I started, mine looked like the Worker's. Now it looks like the Owner's. Which one looks like yours?

Your PFS doesn't lie. It tells you which game you're actually playing.

Your House Is Not a Freedom Asset

For decades, the message has been: "Your home is your biggest investment."

But your primary residence sits on the left side of the Matrix. Part Speculative Wealth (it might appreciate), part Lifestyle Liability (it drains cash every month).

Your house doesn't pay you. It costs you: mortgage, taxes, insurance, repairs, maintenance. Even paid off, the expenses never stop. Appreciation doesn't buy groceries or buy back your time.

A high-earning executive I know bought a $4 million home in California with 20% down. Six months later, he was laid off. That house became a loaded gun pointed at his finances. Huge monthly overhead. No income. No passive cash flow. And the bank wouldn't let him access a dollar of his $800,000 in equity without income.

That's what happens when a Lifestyle Liability wears the costume of a Freedom Asset. The quadrant doesn't change just because the price tag is bigger.

Own a home if it serves your life. I am not saying renting is better than owning. I believe owning is definitely better. Just don't pretend it's building your freedom.

Here's what your primary home actually looks like on a Personal Financial Statement:

Cash Flow Statement

Income (Cash Inflows)	Expenses (Cash Outflows)
	Mortgage Payment *Homeowner's Insurance* *Maintenance & Repairs* *Property Taxes* *Utilities*

Balance Sheet

Assets (Source of Income)	Liabilities (Source of Expenses)
	Primary Home Mortgage

Home Equity Is Trapped Wealth

Your home's equity is part of your net worth. But it doesn't pay you. It doesn't compound by itself. You have no control over it.

Here's what most people never think about: the return on your home equity is 0%.

Your house will appreciate based on the market, not based on how much you've paid off. A $400,000 home that appreciates 4% this year gains $16,000 in value whether you own it outright or have zero equity in it. The appreciation is identical. The only difference is how much of your capital is trapped inside the walls.

Paying extra on your mortgage reduces your debt faster, but it does not increase the asset's return. It does not increase your cash flow. It does nothing but sit there. Yes, you save some future interest. But many people are sitting on mortgages in the 3-7% range. Meanwhile, Freedom Assets can return 10-20% or more annually. You're giving up double or triple the return to save on interest. That's not winning. That's leaving money on the table and calling it responsibility. Worse, every extra dollar you put toward your mortgage is a dollar that could have been buying back your freedom. Paying extra doesn't get you out faster. It keeps you trapped longer.

Every dollar of equity in your primary residence is a dollar not working for you. It's not producing income. It's not compounding. It's not buying back your time.

Would you rather have a paid-off house and work until 65, or redeploy that equity into Freedom Assets and be free in years instead of decades?

Idle equity is dead capital. Redeployed equity becomes an engine.

Retirement Accounts Live on the Left

Your 401(k), IRA, or brokerage account sits in the Speculative Wealth quadrant. They're savings vehicles. Functionally, they're containers you feed money into, hoping the balance grows.

They benefit from Drivers 1, 2, and 3. Freedom Assets benefit from those *and* let you command Driver 4.

To generate meaningful retirement income from these accounts, you need to contribute hundreds of thousands of your own dollars. Every dollar comes from your paycheck. Every dollar requires your time. This is the origin of "it takes money to make money." In this quadrant, it's true.

Your 401(k) might grow 8-12% annually if the market cooperates. A well-operated Freedom Asset can consistently reach 25%+ annual returns when you include cash flow, amortization, appreciation, and forced appreciation through Driver 4. More importantly, you control the outcome.

Use retirement accounts up to the employer match. That's free money, a 100% return. Beyond that, don't depend on them as your freedom strategy.

Freedom Comes from Cash Flow

Net worth is a score. Cash flow is oxygen.

Freedom is built in the top-right quadrant: assets that pay you, grow, and can be improved under your control. The goal isn't to look wealthy on paper. The goal is to build an income engine that replaces your paycheck.

Ask yourself two questions:

1. How many shares of stock can you buy before you run out of money? Whatever's in your checking account.
2. How many Freedom Assets can you buy if they pay you every month and you can use leverage? As many as your skills, investors, and lenders will allow.

That's the shift: from Stage 1 and 2 income, funded by labor, to Stage 4 and 5 income, funded by ownership.

When you stop buying "assets" that behave like liabilities and start owning things that pay you, money stops being your master and starts becoming your soldier. That's when your money enters the Value Loop. And that's when decades become years.

You now have something most people never get: mental models to make sense of reality. You can now see the likely outcome of any financial path before you take it. Most people guess. You won't have to.

The next question is: How do you actually build Freedom Assets faster?

How do you use leverage, arbitrage, tax rules, and other people's money without becoming a slave to any of it?

That's what the next section is about.

The instruments of freedom.

We move from diagnosis to construction.

Turn the page.

Thought Exercise

1. Write down 3 income-producing, appreciating assets you want to explore in the next 2 years.
2. Grab the Personal Financial Statement template in the book bonuses and watch the short walkthrough video to map how your money actually moves. (scan the QR code or visit SterlingSeizert.com/bookbonuses)

PART 4

The Concepts and Instruments of Freedom

CHAPTER 11

Habits of Wealth Creation

Wealth isn't built in one move. It's built in a thousand small ones.

Your habits are the invisible hand steering your financial future. They determine which stage you stay trapped in and which stage you never reach. Stage 1 and 2 habits keep you dependent. Stage 4 and 5 habits create freedom.

The wealthy aren't wealthy because they got lucky. They're wealthy because, over long periods of time, they repeatedly did the unsexy, disciplined, sometimes uncomfortable things that compound.

These habits aren't magical. And they aren't easy. But they work.

I've watched this play out in real time.

Years ago, I worked with two guys at the same company. Same role. Same pay. Same starting line. I've known both of them well for a long time.

We'll call them Chris and Evan.

Chris did what most people do. He lived a normal life. Nice truck. Lifestyle upgrades when raises came. Saved a little. Maxed the company match in his 401(k) and figured the rest would work itself out. He wasn't reckless. He was responsible by middle-class standards. He followed the Accumulation Model and trusted the system.

Evan made a different choice.

Evan decided early that he didn't want to be dependent on a paycheck at 60. He started building the habits in this chapter long before he had money. He saved aggressively, not for "retirement," but for Freedom Assets. He lived below his means on purpose. He read, learned, asked questions, and then started buying income-producing assets. Small at first. Then bigger.

When those assets began producing cash flow, he didn't inflate his lifestyle. He reinvested. Over and over. He and his wife stayed aligned. They delayed some comforts in exchange for control.

After about seven years, Evan put in his two weeks. Not because he hated the job. He actually liked it. But he understood the opportunity cost of staying.

Every hour traded for a paycheck was an hour not spent building, owning, traveling, or being present with his family. When his assets could cover his salary, he chose freedom.

One of his early rewards wasn't a vacation. It was something symbolic.

He purchased another Freedom Asset producing about $1,200 a month in cash flow. Then he bought the truck he'd always wanted with an $800 payment. The asset bought the truck. The remaining $400 kept flowing into the machine. Then he did it again. And again.

Chris is still in the same grind, but he recently went through a major layoff cycle and had to scramble.

Same starting line. Two completely different trajectories.

The difference was in their habits and which system those habits were feeding. Chris fed the Accumulation Trap and hoped it would work out someday. Evan fed Freedom Assets and bought his way out.

I know this story well because I lived both sides of it.

Early on, I was Chris.

I overspent. When young, I wrecked my credit chasing a lifestyle I hadn't earned. As I got older, I still upgraded when I should have saved. I wasn't reckless by most standards. I was normal. And normal kept me stuck.

It took years to dig out of that hole. Years of cleaning up mistakes I didn't have to make. Years of watching money leak into things I can't even remember buying.

That pain is what eventually made me into Evan. I got tired of being owned by my own habits. So I changed them. Slowly. Deliberately. One decision at a time. This sped up my transformation.

The habits in this chapter are the ones that helped create that break from the traditional financial model you already know. They aren't easy, and they aren't even always critical to your success, but they make the journey much easier and faster.

They are what turn knowledge into momentum. They are what turn intention into compounding. They are what allow ordinary people to build extraordinary freedom and control over their time.

What follows are the core habits that separate dependence from freedom. The daily disciplines that allow you to acquire, build, and scale income-producing assets until your life is funded by ownership instead of hours.

Habit 1: Pay Yourself First

Saving money isn't sexy. It doesn't feel powerful. But it is the first act of control.

Everyone knows they should save. That's not the insight. The insight is the order. Most people pay their bills, cover their lifestyle, and save what's left. There's usually nothing left. Owners flip the order. They pay themselves first.

Before the mortgage. Before the car. Before the credit cards. Before groceries. Before comfort. Before lifestyle.

A fixed percentage or amount of your income is pulled out the moment you're paid and moved into a separate bucket with one purpose only: buying freedom.

This is not emergency money. Not vacation money. Not "just in case" money. This is your freedom capital.

People lie to themselves here. They call it savings, but they treat it like a suggestion. They dip into it. They "borrow" from it. Temporary becomes permanent. Then the account meant to fund their escape just ends up feeding the same system they're trapped in.

The discipline is making it untouchable.

At first, it feels like loss. Your brain reads it as restriction. That's the psychology of immediacy. The present always feels louder than the future. That's why people stay stuck in Stage 1 and 2 for decades.

The shift happens when you stop seeing that account as money you can't spend and start seeing it as time you're buying back.

If you struggle saving money, make it automatic.

The moment your paycheck hits, a percentage disappears before you ever see it. The system runs whether you feel disciplined or not.

Start small if you have to. One percent. Twenty bucks. The amount isn't the point. The identity shift and discipline is. Live on that little bit less, then raise your saving a little. A little more with every raise. A little more as expenses drop.

Months will pass. Then a year. One day you look at the account and realize there are thousands of dollars sitting there.

That's your first war chest. Remember I got into my first deal with just $1,500 of my money. This is capital to start learning and to buy your first Freedom Asset.

Without this habit, you'd be in the same place a year later. Same job. Same stress. Just without the capital. The money would have leaked into things you barely remember buying anyway. That was me.

This habit alone won't make you rich. But without it, everything else in this book moves in slow motion.

It's not sexy. It's quiet and slow, but it's foundational for freedom.

Habit 2: Control Expenses

You will never build financial freedom until you control your cash outflows. Not eliminate fun. Not live like a monk. Control.

Every dollar you spend is either feeding your future or feeding the system that keeps you dependent.

This isn't about deprivation. It's about making freedom your priority.

Most people think budgeting is the goal. It's not. Budgeting is survival. I'm not telling you to obsess over your spending. Just plug the unneeded leaks.

The gurus tell you to cut lattes and cancel Netflix like pinching pennies is the path to wealth. That's noise. The wealthy didn't obsess over five-dollar decisions on their rise. They obsessed over where their money flowed and whether it was building assets or funding consumption.

Real freedom doesn't come from cutting your budget; it comes from building income streams that replace your need for one.

The real problem isn't rent or groceries. It's leakage. Small, unnecessary, emotionally driven spending that quietly drains the gap between what you earn and what you could be investing. Dopamine purchases. Convenience upgrades. "I deserve this" spending that feels harmless but compounds in the wrong direction.

The system trains you to consume. Swipe. Feel good. Repeat. Earn and spend. Never build.

Owners play a different game.

They create a gap between income and lifestyle. Not to suffer, but to redirect. That gap is fuel feeding the freedom fund. That gap becomes the down payment, the first deal, the first machine that starts paying them back.

Controlling expenses and paying yourself first just allows you to route more capital into ownership. This can speed up your journey.

Not just to live smaller. But so you can buy bigger. So you can buy your freedom.

Habit 3: Make More Money

Once you've learned to pay yourself first and control your expenses, the next move is obvious: you have to make more money.

Cutting expenses creates the initial gap. Increasing income is what widens it. And widening the gap is what collapses time.

Most people exhaust themselves trying to shrink their life. They try to budget harder. They cut small pleasures. They feel guilty for coffee, dinners out, and anything that looks like enjoyment. Traditional advice turns money into feelings of guilt and constraint.

That's all defense.

You can't win the game by only playing defense.

You can only cut so far before there's nothing left to cut. But income has no ceiling. It can expand indefinitely. That's why *freedom is not a budgeting problem. It's an income problem.*

Once your expenses are under control, it's far easier to earn an extra $2,000 a month than it is to cut another $2,000 out of your life. And that extra $2,000 doesn't just change your savings rate. It changes your options, your confidence, your speed, and your timeline.

Income growth is the accelerator.

Employee Math

Your employer must make more from you than they pay you. If you generate $200,000 in value, they might pay you $90,000 and keep the rest. That's not evil. That's how a business works. But it means your income is capped by someone else's model, someone else's budget, and someone else's ceiling.

A job is not the enemy. I worked one for decades. It can be a powerful tool. But it is still linear. You trade time for money and the upside is limited.

To build real wealth, you eventually need income where you keep most of the value you create.

Maximize the Income You Already Have

Before you chase a side hustle, squeeze the platform you're already standing on.

Most people leave thousands on the table at their day job because they never ask for raises, never document their impact, never solve high-value problems, never move toward performance pay. Not working more hours, but working with more leverage.

Even an extra $5,000–$20,000 a year becomes fuel for buying assets.

Beware the "More School" Trap

Most people think higher income means more credentials. Another degree. Another certification. Another delay. Years of time. Tens of thousands in debt. Slightly higher pay. But they come to find out it's the same treadmill.

That path makes you a better employee, not a wealth builder. Skills that create revenue beat credentials that create resumes.

Add Income You Control

The shift begins here. Income tied to value, not a time clock.

Freelancing. Sales. Commission. Small service businesses. Flipping. Consulting. Digital skills.

Not because you want a "side hustle." Because you want controllable, flexible income that can scale into ownership.

The key is finding something that can grow beyond your direct effort. A service that can be systemized. A skill that can be delegated. A model that can scale from you doing the work to you owning the system. That's how Stage 3 income becomes Stage 4 income.

But here's where many people get stuck. They enter Stage 3 income. More money, more flexibility, more control. And they stay there. They become real estate agents, consultants, loan officers, coaches, freelancers. They make good money. Five years later they're still grinding. Still selling. Still chasing. Still trapped in time-for-money.

They just built themselves a nicer cage.

Stage 3 income is a bridge, not a destination. You don't increase income to upgrade your lifestyle. You increase income to buy Stage 4 systems.

Increase your income. Control where it comes from. Then convert it into machines that produce more income than you ever could. That's how you stop trading hours for dollars and start building engines that buy your time back.

Habit 4: Never Let a Liability Be Paid by Labor

One of the most important sequencing shifts in the entire book.

Most people finally start making more money and immediately upgrade their life. Better car. Bigger house. Nicer trips. They tell themselves they earned it. And maybe they did.

But they make one mistake that quietly locks them into the grind for decades:

They let their labor buy their assets instead of letting their assets buy their lifestyle.

I watched this play out for years. Same company. Same raises. Same bonuses. The moment income went up, spending followed. Nicer truck. Bigger payment. More pressure. More dependence on the next paycheck. No breathing room ever appeared, no matter how much they earned.

Then I learned to ask a different question.

Not "Can I afford this?"

But "What would I have to buy for this to be free?" Same desire, but completely different framing.

Instead of working more hours to pay for a car, a house, or a vacation, you first buy or build something that produces the cash flow to cover it. Then you let that income stream handle the payment. Work hard to buy the asset. Let the asset work hard for your toys.

The order matters. Buy the rental, the business, the storage facility, the equity stake. Let it throw off income. Then use that income to fund the lifestyle.

When you do it this way, three things happen at once:

1. The asset keeps growing in value.
2. The payment eventually ends.
3. The income continues.

This one habit prevents lifestyle creep from trapping you while allowing you to enjoy lifestyle upgrades. It forces every major purchase to pass through a higher standard: not "Can I make the payment?" but "What will pay me while I enjoy this?"

There's nothing wrong with nice things. The mistake is buying them in a way that requires you to keep selling your time to support them.

Freedom comes from building systems that fund your life, not from working harder to maintain it.

The mission is simple: Replace your job income with asset income. Then let asset income buy the life you want.

Not the other way around.

Habit 5: Keep Learning to Create Speed

The biggest difference between people who get free and people who stay stuck isn't intelligence. It's speed of execution.

Not how fast they work. How fast they learn, decide, and move into ownership.

I had a conversation recently that made this painfully clear.

I was mentoring a couple. The husband worked at the fire department. The wife used to work for a firm that handled development planning for large apartment projects. Zoning. Entitlements. Feasibility. Design. She was good at her job and knew how the whole process worked. She helped take raw land and turn it into multimillion-dollar properties.

So I asked her a blunt question.

"How much money did you leave on the table by not being the owner of the projects you helped build?"

She tried to be polite. Said it was hard to calculate. A lot of variables.

So I simplified it.

"Okay. Did you leave millions of dollars on the table by not being the owner?"

She didn't hesitate. "Oh, yeah. Millions."

Let that sink in.

She had the knowledge and the skill. She had the proximity. And she created a massive amount of value.

But she stayed on the salary side of the equation.

She was paid for her time and labor. The owners were paid for ownership.

Same projects. Same buildings. Same outcomes.

Completely different lives.

She didn't lose that money because she took too much risk. She lost out because she stayed on the side of the equation where she never learned how to own the machine. That's what most people get wrong about risk. They think risk is volatility or leverage. It isn't. The real risk is ignorance. Not understanding how value is created. Not understanding how deals work. Not understanding how to protect the downside.

Learning collapses that risk. It turns uncertainty into something you can evaluate, manage, and act on. And the faster you learn, the fewer years and millions you leave on the table.

Most people think education is about becoming smarter or a degree. The wealthy use education to become faster. Faster to see opportunity. Faster to avoid mistakes. Faster to structure deals. Faster to deploy capital. Faster to move from labor to leverage. Faster to move from income to ownership.

I know zero very successful people who didn't have a mentor or coach. Not one.

Yet, the middle class typically tries to figure everything out themselves. They call it being responsible. They call it being cautious. What it really is, most of the time, is paying the tuition of ignorance in years of mistakes, lost opportunities, and compounding.

They will take on $100,000 in student loans without blinking. But they hesitate to invest $5,000 in a mentor, coach, or course that could save them five years of wrong moves.

They will call college an "investment," yet call coaching, courses, and proximity to operators "risky."

That's crazy to me.

The real risk is being slow. The real risk is staying confused. The real risk is learning just enough to be useful to someone else instead of powerful for yourself. The real risk is standing next to the machine and never stepping into the driver's seat.

When I finally paid for mentorship to bring the knowledge I lacked, I didn't just learn tactics. I collapsed time. I avoided deals I would have screwed up. I saw structures I would have missed. I gained confidence that would have taken me years to earn the hard way. I moved from fear and guessing to executing.

The return wasn't just money. It was years of life and freedom. That's what the wealthy are buying when they invest in learning.

Speed. Speed to clarity. Speed to competence. Speed to ownership.

Being ten years late to the life you could have built is the most expensive thing in the world.

Key Takeaways

Once these habits become part of who you are, your trajectory is no longer a mystery. It's math. It's cause and effect.

You are building a machine that can only end in one place: Stage 4 and Stage 5 income. Ownership. Control. Time.

These aren't tips. They're accelerators.

Every one of them shortens the timeline: pay yourself first so your future gets funded before your comfort, control expenses so your money stops leaking, increase income so the gap widens and time collapses, buy assets before liabilities so your life is paid for by machines instead of labor, and keep learning so your speed compounds and your mistakes get cheaper.

This is how freedom is engineered.

You don't need perfection. You need direction. You don't need all of it today. You need the first rep.

Start acting like an owner. Start feeding the machine. Start buying your life back.

Once these habits lock in, the outcome is no longer "if." It's when.

What Comes Next

By now, you've learned the Five Stages of Income, the Freedom Matrix, and why trading time for money keeps people stuck. You've seen the habits that move people out of survival and into freedom. If you want Stage 4 results but you're living with Stage 2 habits, nothing changes.

This is where most readers think: "Okay... but how do I actually start with what I have? How do I afford the assets that will set me free?"

Habits and mindset lay the groundwork, but to move forward, you need a tool that lets you grow beyond the limits of your paycheck. That tool is the same one the wealthy rely on to continue to scale: financial leverage, or debt.

CHAPTER 12

The Debt Paradox

The first time I signed loan documents for an investment property, my hand was shaking.

I was taking on almost five times more debt than I'd ever carried in my life, including my house. Everything I'd been conditioned to believe told me this was reckless. Irresponsible even. The kind of mistake that ruins people. At least that's how the stories were always told. But I'd run the numbers a hundred times. I'd stress tested it. The asset would pay for itself and put money in my pocket every month. The tenants would cover the mortgage. The property would appreciate. And I'd build equity while I slept.

I signed anyway.

That was the moment I realized debt isn't the enemy. Ignorance about debt is.

I believed all debt was bad for most of my adult life. That belief cost me years. The only debt I knew growing up was bad debt: credit cards, car loans, furniture financing. No one showed me the other kind. No one explained that the wealthy use debt as a tool, not a trap.

Debt itself isn't the problem. The real issue is how you use it.

Bad Debt: The Wealth Killer

Bad debt is what most people use. They swipe credit cards for clothes, vacations, furniture, phones, and upgraded cars they can't actually afford. They borrow to consume instead of to create.

I did this for years. Financed a nicer car than I needed. Financed furniture. Bought electronics on a credit card. Told myself I'd pay it off next month. I didn't understand that every one of those decisions was draining my future.

Every dollar spent on bad debt comes from your job. Which means it comes from your time. Every dollar of interest paid on a depreciating purchase is a slice of your life you'll never get back. Bad debt traps people in Stage 1 and Stage 2 because every dollar you owe pulls your time with it.

Bad debt is a financial parasite. It quietly drains your cash flow, shrinks your options, and keeps you chained to the paycheck-to-paycheck treadmill. It's how people end up buying liabilities disguised as assets: bigger houses, nicer cars, lifestyle upgrades that make them look richer while secretly burying them deeper.

Good Debt: The Wealth Builder

Good debt puts money in your pocket. It's used to buy Freedom Assets bigger than you could afford in cash.

Wealth builders take on good debt to buy things like rental properties, businesses, or other income-producing investments. They use money from banks, lenders, or investors to buy assets that produce cash flow and build equity every month without needing all their own capital.

Take a simple rental property: the rent covers the mortgage, taxes, insurance, and maintenance and still leaves monthly profit. The tenant pays down the loan, the property appreciates, and you keep the cash flow and equity. Good debt is the bridge from Stage 2 to Stage 4 because it lets you buy the systems and assets that break the time-for-money equation.

The wealthy understand that debt, when used correctly, isn't risk. It's a tool to acquire assets that produce income.

How Inflation Supercharges Good Debt

Remember what we covered in Chapters 1 and 2: inflation quietly crushes savers. But when you use good debt to buy assets, inflation works for you instead of against you.

Here's how:

You borrow money today at a fixed interest rate. You use that money to buy a cash-flowing, appreciating asset. Then you let inflation, rising prices, and time do the rest.

Let's say you buy a triplex for $650,000 with $150,000 down and a $500,000 loan. Rents bring in $5,700 per month. After all expenses, you net around $700 per month in cash flow.

Now fast-forward 20 years with moderate inflation: The loan shrinks. At 3.5% inflation, the dollar loses half its value in 20 years. Your $500,000 loan feels like $250,000 in today's dollars. Same payment, paid with weaker money.

The property doubles. At 3.5% annual appreciation, your $650,000 property grows to $1,300,000. That's $650,000 in equity created by time, not extra effort.

Rents rise. Your $1,900 per unit rent becomes roughly $3,800. That's $11,400 per month with the same mortgage payment you had on day one. Your net cash flow jumps from $700 to around $5,000 per month.

The loan pays itself down. Over 20 years, tenants pay off roughly $200,000 of your loan balance. That's equity you didn't save or earn. It was built automatically.

End result: You're making $5,000 per month in income and your net worth increased by roughly $850,000. One property. Good debt. Time.

Let those numbers sink in. Net cash flow jumped from $700 to $5,000 per month. Over 600% growth. Total equity grew from $150,000 to roughly $1,000,000. An over 550% increase. You didn't save that money. You didn't grind extra hours. The structure did the work.

Meanwhile, most people spend those same 20 years trying to pay off their house and hoping their retirement account grows.

No one taught you this in school. The math is simple. The strategy is simple. We were all trained to avoid debt, not to understand it. That single misunderstanding is why so many people grind for decades and never break free.

How Workers Use Debt Wrong

I used to fear using debt to build wealth. But I was already using debt all the time, just for the wrong things.

We swipe credit cards at 20% interest without hesitation for stuff that loses value the minute it's purchased, then pay interest on top of the loss. It's a double hit to wealth. First when the thing drops in value, and again when you pay interest on something that's fading. That's how people trap themselves in jobs they can't leave. Yet when someone suggests borrowing to buy a rental property that pays you every month? Suddenly that's "too risky."

It's not the debt itself that's dangerous. It's what you buy with it. If it doesn't produce cash flow, you have to pay for that debt with your job, which means paying for it with your time and labor. That's what robs people of their freedom.

The Worker mindset is: "How will I pay this back?"

The Owner mindset is: "How will an asset pay this for me?"

Used for liabilities, debt is a trap. Used for assets, debt is a lever.

The Bigger Picture

Good debt is one form of leverage. But leverage is bigger than borrowing.

The next chapter shows you how to use all five forms of leverage to control assets, scale income, and build freedom faster than your bank account alone would ever allow.

Turn the page.

Thought Exercise:

1. Write down two or three of your bad debts that you need to eliminate from your balance sheet.
2. Write down one good debt you can add: an investment that will put money in your pocket every month.
3. Go to your book bonuses from the beginning of the book or end of Chapter 7 and get your PFS filled out.

CHAPTER 13

The Secret of Leverage and Arbitrage

I bought an 18-unit apartment building with $1,500 of my own money.

The purchase price was $900,000. I didn't have the cash. I didn't have the resume. What I had was the deal. Rents were low, operations were sloppy, and the seller was tired.

Two investors funded the $300,000 down payment. The seller financed $600,000. No bank. No underwriting. My wife and I ran the asset, improved operations, raised rents, and eventually handed the day-to-day to a property management company.

A few years later, we sold it for $1,825,000. Our investors earned a 40% compound annualized return. We walked away with life-changing money.

That deal was only possible because I understood leverage.

Leverage is more than borrowing money. It's using less of your own resources to control more of the outcome. There are five forms. Master them and you can build wealth faster than your bank account alone would ever allow.

The Five Forms of Leverage

1. Financial Leverage

This is what most people think of when they hear "leverage." Using other people's money to control assets bigger than your cash would allow.

Banks, seller financing, private lenders, equity partners. These are the tools already built into the financial system. The wealthy use them constantly. You can too.

You don't have to bring all the money. You bring the deal, the plan, or the effort. You borrow the rest.

In my 18-unit deal, two investors supplied the capital. The seller financed the majority of the purchase. I supplied the deal, the structure, and the operations. Financial leverage let me control a $900,000 asset with $1,500 of my own money.

Remember the Four Drivers of Appreciation from Chapter 8? Only the fourth driver, operational performance, creates real freedom. Financial leverage amplifies that driver. When you use leverage to acquire a Freedom Asset, income growth doesn't just put more money in your pocket. It multiplies your equity. It accelerates your net worth. It lets you buy more assets, faster, without using all your own money.

Leverage moves you from Stage 1 and 2 income into Stage 4 and 5. Almost no one reaches financial freedom quickly without it.

2. Knowledge Leverage

Skill is equity.

Every successful deal runs on five components: the deal itself, capital, bankability, asset management skills, and day-to-day operations. You don't need all five. You just need one. Bring what you have. Borrow what you don't.

The deal itself is the most powerful. Money chases great deals, not the other way around. In my 18-unit deal, this is what I brought. I found the property, ran the numbers, negotiated the terms. That skill earned me equity even though I had almost no cash.

If you don't have money, get good at finding deals. It's the highest-ROI skill you can develop.

Capital is what beginners obsess about. But it's only one piece. Capital covers the down payment, closing costs, reserves, and renovation funds. You don't have to supply it to control the deal. Money can come from partners, investors, creative financing, or seller equity.

Bankability means meeting the requirements for traditional loans. Banks look at net worth, liquidity, credit, and experience. I didn't have bankability on my first deal. So I structured around it. When the deal is structured creatively, bankability becomes optional.

Asset management is where real wealth is created. This means implementing the business plan: raising rents, cutting expenses, supervising renovations, optimizing operations, increasing income. In my deal, this was another lever I brought. My wife and I improved operations and raised rents. That skill earned us more ownership stake, even though the capital came from elsewhere.

The rule: The more factors you bring, the more equity you earn, typically with less of your own money. The fewer you bring, the more you give to others.

You don't need all five factors. You only need one. Don't get greedy. Get the deal done. It's better to own part of a watermelon than a whole grape.

3. People Leverage

You can't scale alone.

Partners bring what you lack. Investors bring capital. Operators bring execution. Teams and employees run the machine without you.

In my first deal, I had partners who funded the down payment. I didn't try to do it all myself. I found people whose strengths filled my gaps, and we all won.

As you grow, people leverage becomes essential. Property managers handle tenants so you don't. Employees run operations so you can focus on acquisition. Contractors execute renovations so you're not swinging a hammer.

The goal isn't to do everything yourself. The goal is to build something that works without you doing everything. That's Stage 4. That's freedom.

4. Systems Leverage

Systems are processes that scale without your presence.

Day-to-day operations. Leasing. Collections. Maintenance. Tenant experience. Bookkeeping. Marketing.

Whether you do it yourself or hire a management company, these systems keep the income flowing without costing you all your time.

In the beginning, you might run the systems yourself. That's fine. But the goal is to build processes that can be handed off. Documented. Repeated. Improved by others.

Systems leverage is what turns Stage 3 income into Stage 4. Your effort builds the machine. The machine runs without your constant effort. That's the difference between owning a job and owning a business.

5. Time Leverage

Build once, get paid forever.

The wealthy invest weeks structuring a deal that pays them for decades. One move, executed well, can create a lifetime of income.

Meanwhile, most people spend 40 hours a week chasing dollars that vanish the moment the bills clear.

Time leverage means your work compounds. You're not starting over every month. Every deal you close, every system you build, every asset you acquire adds to the machine. The income stacks. The equity grows. The effort you put in today keeps paying you tomorrow.

This connects back to the Value Loop. Income creates equity. Equity funds acquisition. Acquisition creates new income. Each asset runs its own loop. The loops multiply. That's time leverage at scale.

Financial Leverage in Action: Real Estate

Most people never invest in real estate because they think they don't have enough money. Coming up with $400,000 in cash is nearly impossible for most. So they stay on the sidelines.

The problem isn't that real estate is out of reach. It's that people believe they need to buy in cash to be safe. That thinking keeps them stuck while the wealthy use leverage to scale faster and build wealth exponentially.

Let's compare two options using the same $400,000. Before you think "I don't have $400,000," stay with me. This is about understanding how leverage multiplies returns. Once you see it, you'll understand why the wealthy use it at every level, and how you can access it starting with far less.

Scenario: Buy One Property or Buy Four

You've been told buying in cash is safest. No debt, no mortgage payments, full ownership from day one. So you find a duplex for $400,000, buy it outright, and start collecting rent.

But what if you used that same $400,000 as down payments to acquire four duplexes instead?

Metric	Scenario 1: Buy One Property	Scenario 2: Buy Four Properties
Total Properties Owned	1	4
Total Asset Value Controlled	$400,000	$1,600,000
Total Down Payment	$400,000	$400,000
Total Loan Amount	$0	$1,200,000
Monthly Mortgage Payment	$0	$8,000
Annual Appreciation Growth (5%)	$20,000	$80,000
ROI on Appreciation	5%	20%
Monthly Rent Received per Property	$3,800	$3,800
Total Rent Received	$3,800	$15,200
Total Expenses (Mortgage, Taxes, Insurance, etc)	$1,000	$12,000
Net Monthly Cash Flow (CF)	$2,800	$3,200
Annual Net Cash Flow	$33,600	$38,400
Cash -on-Cash Return (Annual Cash flow / Down Payment)	8.4%	9.6%
Annual Loan Paydown (Rate: 7%)	$0	$12,190
Total Cash Plus Equity Gained (Appreciation+CF+ Paydown)	$53,600	$130,590
Total Annual ROI (Appreciation+Cash Flow+Loan Paydown)	13.4%	32.6%

Why Leverage Wins

Same money, 4X the growth. With 5% appreciation, the cash purchase gets you $20,000 in equity. Four leveraged properties earn $80,000.

More than double your ROI. Cash gets you 13.4%. Leverage gets you 32.6%.

Tenants pay your mortgage. With leverage, tenants cover $8,000 per month in loan payments. A portion becomes your equity every month.

More cash flow. The leveraged approach brings in $3,200 per month net, more than the $2,800 per month from buying in cash, despite having mortgages.

Inflation works for you. Your mortgage stays fixed while rents rise. A $50 rent increase across all units gains you $200 per month with four properties versus $50 with one.

By leveraging wisely, you multiply returns, scale faster, and let money work for you.

Financial Leverage in Action: Business

Most people think buying a business requires writing a massive check. It doesn't. Businesses are bought every day using seller financing, SBA loans, investor capital, and earnouts. The buyer brings the deal, the plan, and the ability to operate. The money comes from elsewhere.

Here's a simple example:

You find a small service business doing $500,000 in annual revenue with $150,000 in profit. The owner wants to retire and agrees to sell for $300,000, a 2x multiple. Instead of paying cash, you negotiate $30,000 down and $270,000 seller-financed over five years at 6%.

Your annual debt payment is about $64,000. The business profits $150,000. After debt service, you keep roughly $86,000 per year in cash flow, and you're building equity with every payment. In five years, you own the business free and clear.

You just bought $86,000 in annual income with $30,000 down. That's a 287% cash-on-cash return.

This isn't passive. You'll need to run the business or hire someone who can. But remember you don't need all five factors of a deal. You just need one. In this example, your knowledge and effort are the leverage. That's why the returns are so high. When you bring skill to the table, you don't need as much money.

The vehicle doesn't matter. The principles do. Leverage lets you control assets bigger than your bank account. Whether it's a service business, a hybrid like storage facilities or laundromats, or real estate like apartments and duplexes, the math works the same way.

Arbitrage: Profiting from the Spread

Arbitrage is the quiet engine behind every major financial institution, real estate empire, and business success.

At its core, arbitrage is simple: make money on the spread between what something costs you and what it pays you.

Borrow money at 5%, put it to work earning 10%, and that 5% gap is yours to keep. That's arbitrage. Scale it, and it becomes unstoppable.

Simple Example:

A trusted friend asks to borrow $1,000. They agree to pay you back $1,100 at the end of the year, a 10% return.

Instead of using your own money, you borrow the $1,000 from the bank at 5% interest.

At the end of the year, you pay the bank $1,050. Your friend pays you $1,100. You keep the $50 profit, without using any of your own money.

You just created money using arbitrage. This isn't a life-changing example, but I want you to understand the concept. When you scale it, it will change your life.

How Banks Use Arbitrage

This concept has a name: fractional reserve banking.

When you deposit $10,000, the bank doesn't keep it sitting in a vault. They keep a fraction in reserves and lend out the rest. That loan becomes someone else's deposit, which gets lent out again. Your original $10,000 can expand into $90,000 or more in total loans.

The bank pays you 2% on your deposit and earns 7% on the loans they created from it. They pocket the spread. They make money on funds they don't even own, and then they tell you debt is dangerous and leverage is irresponsible.

Banks, hedge funds, and the wealthy already operate this way. They borrow at one rate, invest at a higher rate, and profit from the spread. Every single day.

Once you understand how arbitrage works, you can stop being the customer and start playing the game.

How You Use Arbitrage

You find a rental property earning 9% if you buy in cash. Instead, you finance it with a loan at 6%. The 3% spread is your profit. Depending on deal size, this pays you hundreds, thousands, or even tens of thousands monthly without using your own money.

That 3% might not sound like much. But scale it:

- $400,000 financed = $12,000 per year
- $1.6 million = $48,000 per year
- $4 million = $120,000 per year
- $8 million = $240,000 per year
- $15 million = $450,000 per year

So, if your freedom number is $10,000 per month, you don't need a miracle. You need a portfolio capturing a 3% spread on about $4 million in financing. Or a 2% spread on $6 million. The spread is what matters. And, if the deal makes sense, the bank, partners, or investors bring the money.

Freedom isn't built by grinding for 40 years and saving more. It's built by learning how money works and making it work for you.

The Real Difference

In the Accumulation Trap, your money is the only engine. You work. You save. You invest what you can set aside. Your progress is limited by the size of your own pile because financial leverage isn't part of the model.

In the Ownership Model, your capital isn't the primary engine. Structure is.

You're not trying to earn 8% on just your own savings. You're trying to control assets that pay you a spread on money you didn't have to save.

One path requires you to accumulate hundreds of thousands of your own dollars before the math works. The other lets you build income now using deals, leverage, and other people's capital.

One is slow, linear, and capped by your paycheck. The other is scalable and limited only by your ability to find and structure good opportunities.

Same destination. Completely different timeline

When Leverage Turns Against You

Everything I've shown you about leverage is true. It multiplies returns. It compresses timelines. It builds wealth faster than saving ever could.

It also multiplies mistakes.

If you over-leverage, buy too much, too fast, with too little margin, a vacancy spike, a rate increase, or an economic contraction can wipe you out. I've seen it happen. Good operators with bad timing or thin reserves who lost everything because the math that worked at 95% occupancy collapsed at 75%.

The wealthy don't just use leverage. They manage it. They stress-test every deal. What happens if vacancy doubles? What if rates jump 2%? What if I can't refinance for three years? If the deal still survives, it's a deal. If it doesn't, walk away.

My rule: never let leverage put you in a position where one bad quarter forces a sale. Reserves aren't optional. Conservative loan-to-value isn't weakness. Stress-testing isn't pessimism. These are the guardrails that let you use leverage aggressively.

Leverage is a power tool. Respect it, or it'll take your hand off.

What Comes Next

Leverage isn't about taking more risk. It's about using less of yourself to control more of the outcome.

But mention leverage or debt to most people and they freeze. They've been taught that risk means danger. That playing it safe means staying small.

The next chapter reframes risk entirely. Because the biggest risk isn't using leverage. It's staying dependent on a system you don't control.

Turn the page.

CHAPTER 14

Rethinking Risk

Susan had a great job. Six figures. Good benefits. Promotions lined up. She did everything "right." College degree. Bought a house. Maxed out her 401(k) every year. Drove a modest car. Followed the plan.

Then one phone call changed everything.

"Your position has been eliminated."

No warning. No fault of her own. And just like that, her income was gone. The "safe" path? Vaporized.

This story isn't rare. It's happening every day. Economic shutdowns, policy shifts, corporate downsizing, AI replacing roles. Most people are one decision made in a boardroom away from losing everything they depend on.

Yet we're taught to fear the opposite things. Buying a business. Buying real estate. Investing outside the stock market. We've been conditioned to think those are risky. But risk isn't in doing something unconventional. Risk is in relying completely on things you don't control.

Susan did everything right according to the rules. But the rules were never written to protect her.

The Truth About Risk

Risk isn't a number. It's not volatility. It's not debt.

When you really think about it, risk is simply a lack of predictability. *And predictability is just a function of knowledge and control.*

If you don't know what's going to happen, or how to influence the outcome, then yes, it feels risky. But the moment you increase your knowledge, sharpen your skills, and take control of the situation, risk drops dramatically.

The core truth most people never learn: risk isn't fixed. It's variable. And you control the variables.

Workers avoid "risky" moves because they were never taught how to make financial outcomes predictable. They hand their life savings to a financial planner who puts it in a system that even they can't control. The wealthy view that as the riskiest move of all.

The wealthy don't avoid risk. They study how to make outcomes predictable. Then they act.

You Don't Fear Investing. You Fear Not Knowing.

Most people say they're afraid of "risk." But that's not actually true.

Nobody is born afraid of real estate. Nobody is born afraid of starting a business. What you really fear is your own ignorance. You fear what you don't understand, so the unknown feels dangerous.

You don't fear the investment. You fear your lack of knowledge about it. You don't fear the debt. You fear your lack of control. You don't fear the opportunity. You fear whether you can handle it.

Fear is not a signal to avoid something. Fear is a signal telling you where to learn next.

Here's what's crazy: most people spend 16+ years in school just to qualify for a job to earn money. Then they spend zero time learning how money actually works. They study for years to earn an income, but never study how to keep it, grow it, or multiply it.

That's the real risk. Ignorance is the most expensive form of risk there is.

The solution is self-education. Not another degree. Books. Courses. Mentors. Coaching. Proximity to people who have done what you want to do. This is how you learn to find, structure, and buy Freedom Assets. They don't teach this in college. They teach you to be an employee.

Once you replace ignorance with knowledge and uncertainty with control, the fear dissipates. What once looked "risky" suddenly becomes obvious, logical, predictable.

The Risk You Don't See Coming: Yourself

Once you stop outsourcing decisions and start taking control, risk doesn't disappear. It changes shape. The market is no longer the biggest threat. At that point, the most dangerous risk is much closer.

It's you. This is execution risk. Knowing what to do but failing to do it well.

I learned this on my very first deal: that 18-unit apartment building in Colorado Springs. Two investors funded the $300,000 down payment. I negotiated seller financing on the balance. My wife and I managed the property ourselves. The asset performed. It cash-flowed. On paper, everything was working.

Then one afternoon, I logged into the operating account. The balance was zero.

Not low. Zero.

My stomach dropped. I called my wife. She hadn't moved anything. We ran through every possibility: fraud, a bank error, something we'd missed. Then we called our partners.

They had moved the money. All of it. Into a separate account we didn't have access to.

Why? Because they thought we were stealing from the partnership.

We weren't. Not a dollar had been taken. But after the initial shock, I understood immediately how it looked from their seat.

I had been so focused on operations that I neglected something basic: communication. I wasn't sending clear, consistent reports. I wasn't documenting expenses in a way that was easy to follow. I assumed performance spoke for itself.

It doesn't.

From their perspective, all they saw was money going out and silence coming back. That's a vacuum people fill with fear.

I spent the next several days outlining the paper trail. Every receipt, every invoice, every expense. We walked through it together. They saw the truth. Nothing dishonest had happened.

The deal survived. We eventually sold that property for nearly double what we paid. But the lesson wasn't about money.

I had done the hard parts right: finding the deal, structuring it, raising capital, operating the asset. But I almost killed the entire thing because I failed at something unglamorous: keeping people informed.

Risk doesn't live in markets first. It lives in assumptions. The most dangerous assumption is believing other people see what you see.

Since then, I over-communicate by default. Trust is infrastructure. Without it, no deal, no system, no strategy holds for long.

The Hidden Risks Hiding in Plain Sight

Most people obsess over the risks of buying a rental property or starting a business. Yet they never question the slow, silent risks bleeding them dry every day. These feel normal. That's what makes them dangerous.

Every one of them comes back to the same problem: lack of knowledge, lack of control, or both.

Relying on one income source. You have no control over whether that paycheck continues. One recession, one policy change, one management shuffle. You're exposed and don't even see it.

Trusting an employer or the government to protect your future. You're depending on someone else's competence and incentives. You have no knowledge of their real plans and no control over their decisions.

Taking financial advice from people who aren't financially free. You're borrowing knowledge from people who don't have the results you want. That's not education. That's the blind leading the blind.

Hoping assets appreciate instead of building cash flow. You have no control over market sentiment. You're gambling on forces outside your influence instead of building income you command.

These risks don't feel like risks because they're familiar. But apply the test: Do you have knowledge of the outcome? Do you have control over it? If the answer is no to both, you're exposed.

The solution is always the same. Increase your knowledge. Take back control.

The Responsibility Inversion

We're taught that handing our financial future to professionals is the responsible thing to do.

But think about what that actually means. The advisor has the knowledge. The institution has the control. You have neither. You're hoping they're honest. Hoping they're competent. Hoping the market cooperates. Hoping you don't get laid off before you're ready.

That's not responsibility. That's abdication dressed up as prudence.

The definitions got flipped somewhere along the way. Blind trust got labeled "safe." Taking ownership got labeled "risky."

Real irresponsibility is handing your family's future to strangers with misaligned incentives, then telling yourself you made the safe choice.

Real responsibility is owning the outcome. Building the knowledge yourself. Taking control of your income, your assets, your decisions. Learning how to make outcomes predictable instead of hoping someone else does it for you.

If you're reading this book, you've probably felt the tension. Part of you knows the traditional path isn't working. But another part feels guilty for questioning it, like you're being reckless for even considering something different.

You're not being reckless. You're waking up.

No one is coming to save you. The longer you wait, the more power you give away. The safest path isn't staying where you are. It's becoming someone who creates predictable outcomes through knowledge and control.

That's not risky. That's freedom.

Thought Exercise:

1. What happens if you lose your job tomorrow?
2. Who are you depending on right now?
3. Who is depending on you right now?
4. What are you risking by doing nothing?

CHAPTER 15

The Power of Ownership and Control

I once paid a company to build and run an Amazon store for me. On paper, it was perfect: automated, scalable, low effort. They handled everything. I'd sit back and collect the cash.

Until one of their virtual assistants botched an invoice. Amazon flagged it. Instead of a quick fix, the team fumbled the response – twice. My store was shut down. We tried launching another. Same story. Another failure.

Not because Amazon doesn't work. Because I had zero control over the outcome. I didn't understand the systems. I couldn't step in and fix the problem. My entire investment depended on someone else's competence, and they failed me.

That was my fault. I had invested in something I didn't understand and couldn't influence.

That experience codified the rule: never blindly put your financial future in someone else's hands.

Delegation without understanding is not leverage. It's dependency.

That's the difference between someone who hopes for the best and an Owner who builds control.

Ownership Is the Path

In the last chapter, we defined risk as a lack of predictability. Predictability comes from knowledge and control. Ownership is how you create it. Control is how you protect it.

Workers work for money. Owners make money work for them.

You already know this from the Freedom Matrix. Ownership of income-producing machines is the basis of freedom. Whether it's real estate, a business, or intellectual property, the pattern is always the same: you build something that pays you whether you're working or not.

But ownership alone isn't enough. The Amazon store was something I owned. What I didn't have was control. That's the distinction this chapter is about.

Control Is What Protects It

Most people misunderstand effort. They think wealth requires more work. It doesn't. People already work hard. They wake up early, commute, sit in meetings, deal with stress, and give forty to fifty hours a week to someone else's machine.

The problem isn't effort. It's where the effort goes.

Effort applied inside a system you don't own or control has a ceiling. No matter how hard you work, the upside belongs to someone else. That's why employees can grind for decades and still feel capped. That's the Worker's trap: trading harder work for the same limited outcome.

Effort without control is a treadmill.

Once you own and control the system, effort changes character. The same hours you'd spend at a job now build equity, increase cash flow, and expand options. Improving pricing, operations, or decision-making directly increases income and long-term value. Every hour invested compounds.

The difference between busy hours and impact hours. Busy hours keep someone else's machine running. Impact hours build yours. When you direct effort toward assets in the Freedom Asset quadrant, your skills and effort compound over time. We'll go deeper on this in Chapter 22.

Escaping often takes less effort than staying trapped. People give their best hours to someone else's machine but hesitate to invest a few focused hours a week into their own, because now the outcome is on them.

When you work for someone else, responsibility is limited. Show up, do the job, get paid. When you own the system, responsibility is total. Wins are yours. Losses are yours. No one else to blame.

But that responsibility is where freedom comes from.

Why the Market Doesn't Give You Control

I don't trust the stock market with my future.

I can't call the CEO of Apple and ask them to change course. I can't stop Disney from tanking their brand with bad decisions. I'm along for the ride, watching my net worth rise and fall based on what other people do.

Remember the Four Drivers from Chapter 8. Most stock market gains come from Drivers 1, 2, and 3 – inflation, supply and demand, investor sentiment. All outside your influence. All capable of vanishing overnight.

None of them raise your freedom. As investor Howard Marks wrote in Mastering the Market Cycle:

"Investors rarely maintain objective, rational, neutral, and stable positions. First, they exhibit high levels of optimism, greed, risk tolerance, and credulousness... But then, for some reason, perhaps the arrival of a tipping point, they switch to pessimism, fear, risk aversion, and skepticism."

That's not a strategy. That's handing your future to crowd psychology.

The average investor is along for the ride, hoping it doesn't crash right before they retire.

Stocks can be part of a portfolio. They cannot be the foundation of freedom. Freedom requires control. Control requires owning assets you can actually influence.

Control Starts with Financial Literacy

So what's the solution?

You take ownership. You build control. And you do it by building knowledge and skills.

That doesn't mean going back to school. You don't need an MBA. Control begins the moment you can read a financial statement, underwrite an asset, and make a decision without asking permission.

Once you understand how the numbers work, you'll want control.

The moment you understand how real estate works, you'll stop fearing it. The moment you learn how to analyze a business, you'll stop settling for a job. The moment you realize what leverage really means, you'll start looking at money like a tool, not a goal.

Workers avoid control because they don't feel ready. Owners seek control because they've built the knowledge and confidence to handle it.

The gap between them isn't talent. It's decision.

Ownership Is Tax-Advantaged

The tax code rewards ownership. Most people never realize this because they only know one type of income: earned income. Trading time for money through a job. It's also the most heavily taxed.

Earned income gets hit with federal income tax (up to 37%), payroll taxes (7.65%), and state and local taxes (0-15% depending on where you live). The more you earn, the more they take. The government gets paid before you do.

But there are two other types of income the tax code treats very differently.

Portfolio income comes from stocks, bonds, and mutual funds. Long-term capital gains are taxed at 0%, 15%, or 20%. Better than a paycheck, but you can't write off expenses or depreciate a stock portfolio. You have no control.

Passive income comes from assets and systems that work for you: rental properties, royalties, business distributions. This is where ownership pays off. No payroll taxes. Depreciation deductions that reduce taxable income even while the asset appreciates. Expenses come off the top before you pay a dime in taxes.

Here's what that looks like in practice. Say you own a rental property that produces $24,000 a year in net cash flow. You'd think you owe taxes on $24,000. But depreciation on the building – a paper deduction, no actual money spent – might offset $15,000 or more of that income. You'd only pay taxes on $9,000 of real income while pocketing all $24,000. Meanwhile, a W-2 employee earning $24,000 in overtime pays taxes on every dollar before they see it. Same income. Completely different tax treatment.

Most people follow this formula:

Earn → Pay Taxes → Spend What's Left

Owners flip the order:

Earn → Spend Pre-Tax Dollars → Pay Taxes on What's Left

That's not a loophole. That's how the tax code is designed. The government wants people to create jobs, provide housing, and build businesses. So it rewards those who do.

The U.S. tax code is nearly 7,000 pages long. Less than 10% details what you owe. The other 90% explains how to reduce your bill through deductions, exemptions, and credits.

Employees are taxed the highest. Owners are taxed the least. If you want to keep more, you have to switch sides.

As you scale, you'll add legal structures like LLCs, corporations, and trusts that protect what you've built. The wealthy control everything but own nothing personally. One lawsuit can't take down an empire that's properly structured.

Start simple. One LLC for your first asset. Add layers as you grow. But understand this from day one: ownership isn't just how you build wealth. It's how you keep it.

Ownership Is the Territory. Control Is the High Ground.

When you own the asset, you own the upside.

When you control the asset, you protect the downside.

When you build the knowledge to do both, you don't fear the future. You shape it.

The next chapter shows you why focus, not diversification, is how you get there faster.

CHAPTER 16

Focus Is Better Than Diversification

You've been lied to: "Spread your money around. Don't put all your eggs in one basket. Diversify and you'll be safe."

That's the script they feed us our whole lives. It sounds smart. It sounds responsible. But it's exactly why most people stay trapped in a job and never build real wealth.

Diversification doesn't make you rich. It keeps you average. It keeps you stuck in your cubicle. It's a safety net for people who don't know what they're doing. Warren Buffett didn't mince words:

"Diversification is protection against ignorance."

Remember how we defined risk: a lack of predictability. Predictability comes from knowledge and control. Focus is how you build both.

To diversify is to admit you don't have knowledge or control over the outcome. It's not how you build wealth. It's how you hedge risk when you don't have a clue. If you want to build wealth, you don't spread out. You lock in and go deep.

Study any self-made millionaire or billionaire and you'll notice a pattern: none of them built their wealth by diversifying into index funds and waiting. Buffett went deep into undervalued businesses he could control. Bezos poured everything into one company until it dominated. Musk reinvested every dollar from PayPal into the next venture.

For every Bezos, there are thousands of focused entrepreneurs who went broke. Focus alone doesn't guarantee success. But focus guarantees depth of knowledge and experience, and that depth is the only thing that gives you control over outcomes.

That's why focus matters. Not because it eliminates failure, but because it's the prerequisite for Driver 4. You can't force appreciation on an asset you barely understand. Mastery gives you the knowledge that makes leverage safe and compounding possible.

The guy in your town with 500 apartments didn't get there by spreading $500 across ten different strategies. He got there by learning one game cold and playing it over and over.

Wealth isn't built by spreading risk. It's built through focused mastery, strategic execution, and control.

Diversification Is for Preserving Wealth

There's a time for diversification, but it's not at the beginning. Diversification is a wealth-preservation strategy, not a wealth-building one.

You don't diversify to get rich. You diversify after you're rich to stay rich.

That's why they call them wealth management firms, not wealth creation firms. They can't help you turn $20,000 into $2 million or $100,000 into $10 million in five to fifteen years. That kind of growth only comes from focus and ownership.

Focus to get rich. Diversify to stay rich.

Why Focus Wins

Diversified, passive investing, like dollar-cost averaging into index funds, might sound smart until you run the numbers. Even if you locked in a perfect 12% annual return, year after year, which no fund manager on Wall Street has ever pulled off consistently, you'd still wait 20 years to turn $100,000 into $1 million. More realistically, 30 years or longer.

And that's the real problem: you can't speed it up. You can't work harder, get better, or make sharper decisions, because the system doesn't reward any of that. You have no control. No leverage. No way to create value through your own knowledge and effort. No way to accelerate the outcome.

Focus changes that equation entirely. When you go deep in one asset class, every hour of effort compounds into deeper knowledge and sharper instincts. By year five, you see opportunities others miss. You know the game. You know the players. You know the moves. You stack win after win because your experience is building on itself.

Split your capital across ten investments and you'll master none of them. Even if one hits big, you won't have enough in it to change your life. Jump from strategy to strategy and you never build momentum. You stay in beginner mode forever.

I've lived both sides. Every time I lost money, it was because I got distracted or stepped into something I didn't fully understand. Every time I made money, it was because I focused, built expertise, and doubled down on what I knew.

Workers diversify out of fear. The wealthy focus because they know mastery eliminates risk. Going all-in doesn't mean gambling on one coin flip. It means choosing a lane and mastering it before you expand. It means building deep knowledge instead of shallow familiarity. That's what turns "risk" into predictability and opportunity into profit.

Focus gives you knowledge. Knowledge gives you control. Control builds wealth. Compounding favors the focused.

Study the Map. Choose Your Route.

You can, and should, study different paths. Real estate. Business. Storage. Short-term rentals. Buying service companies. Learn what's out there. Figure out what speaks to you. Once something clicks, lock in.

Pick the asset class or strategy that fits you and go deep. Read everything. Study the players. Learn the language. Talk to operators. Walk deals. Take notes. Build your edge.

General knowledge gets you curious. Specialized knowledge makes you rich.

Find your lane and master it.

PART 5

Building Your Freedom Machine

CHAPTER 17

Choose Your Freedom Asset

You've now completed Part 4. You understand the instruments of financial freedom. You know how to break the time-for-money trap, use debt strategically, leverage other people's money, manage risk, take ownership and control, focus your efforts, and protect what you build.

Now comes the real question: What are you going to build?

The Three Paths to Financial Freedom

Only three viable paths lead to financial freedom. Every strategy, every guru, every book falls into one of these categories.

The Accumulation Model. This is the default. Max your 401(k). Diversify into index funds. Live below your means. Wait 30-40 years. Hope the math works out. It's the path most people follow because it's the only one they've been taught. It can work eventually, but it's slow, you have no control, and your outcome depends entirely on market performance and timing. You spend your best years waiting.

The FIRE Movement. FIRE stands for Financial Independence, Retire Early. It's really just the Accumulation Model on fast-forward. Cut expenses to the bone. Save 50-70% of your income. Invest aggressively in index funds. Retire in 10-15 years instead of 40. It works for the disciplined few, but it requires extreme sacrifice during your prime years. And once you "retire," you're still dependent on a safe withdrawal rate, market returns, and a lean budget. You're free, but fragile.

Freedom Assets. This is the path of ownership. You build or buy income-producing machines you control. Cash flow replaces your paycheck. Not someday, but progressively, as you acquire assets. You benefit from all Four Drivers of Appreciation, especially Driver 4, which you command. Your wealth compounds through effort, skill, and reinvestment. You don't wait for freedom. You build it.

The first two paths share the same fundamental flaw: dependence. Your outcome relies on forces outside your control. Market returns, inflation, sequence of returns risk, withdrawal rates. You're a passenger.

The Freedom Assets path is different. You're the operator. You control income. You control value. You control the timeline.

This book is about the third path.

What Freedom Actually Requires

People don't get rich working a job, then investing in stocks. They get rich by building or buying a machine that throws off cash and keeps growing. They create or fix something that produces income while they sleep. Sometimes that takes years. Sometimes it happens fast. But the pattern is always the same: owning one or more Freedom Assets that create Stage 4 or Stage 5 income while benefiting from all Four Drivers of Appreciation.

Workers spend their lives feeding someone else's machine. Owners build their own.

Every paycheck you've ever earned came from someone else's Stage 4 or 5 Freedom Asset. A machine you didn't own. The question is whether the rest of your life will be the same. And whether your children will inherit ownership or dependence.

If you want real wealth, you eventually have to stop renting your time and start owning the machine.

Part 5 is where we go from instruments to assets. From theory to selection. From understanding why wealth-building works to choosing the machine that will carry you from financial survival to financial freedom.

This part of the book shows you how each Freedom Asset fits the frameworks from Part 3. You'll see how the Five Stages, the Freedom Matrix, the Four Drivers, and the Freedom Asset Test apply to real businesses and real estate. This is not a complete guide to acquisition or deal-making. Those topics fill entire libraries. What follows is enough to understand how each asset functions, what makes it work, and which path fits you. Once you know where you're leaning, you go deeper through books, courses, and mentors specific to your chosen lane. This is the map. Execution requires more.

The Three Types of Machines

Three primary types of Freedom Asset machines build real wealth. They sit in the top-right quadrant of the Freedom Matrix and benefit from all Four Drivers, especially Driver 4 when you operate them well.

Each type passes the Freedom Asset test: they produce cash flow, give you control, allow leverage, let you create value, work with the tax code, and resist inflation. The difference is how they scale, how much involvement they require, and which skills they reward.

The Business Machine

A couple who are neighbors of ours were stuck in the grind. He was a physician assistant working two jobs just to keep up. She had been laid off when her non-profit cut staff. They were exhausted and going nowhere.

They decided to go for it. She built a home-visit pediatric healthcare business from scratch. Found a doctor to bring on for licensing. Set up the operations, the scheduling, the billing. Within a year, they're about to replace the income from both his jobs. Now they're bringing on more PAs and doctors to scale it.

They didn't invent anything. They found existing demand. Parents who want healthcare that comes to them. Then they built a machine to serve it. That's the pattern.

Others do the same with digital businesses. MJ DeMarco built a limo booking website that connected customers with limo companies. Simple problem, digital solution, recurring transactions. He scaled it, systematized it, and sold it for millions. Some buy underperforming software businesses or agencies, then apply Driver 4: improve operations, reduce churn, raise prices, systematize delivery. The business was already producing income. They just made it produce more.

New categories emerge constantly. Businesses helping other companies automate operations, manage their marketing, or adopt new technology. Someone learns digital advertising, funnel building, or AI automation, then starts or acquires an agency serving that need. The specific opportunity changes. The pattern doesn't: find demand, build or buy the machine, improve it, scale it.

Business machines also include service-based companies like HVAC, plumbing, landscaping, and vending routes. These aren't glamorous. But the income they produce is. They solve real problems. They're simple. They're repeatable. They can be built from scratch or acquired, then scaled with systems and people.

Business machines typically produce higher cash-on-cash returns than most other Freedom Assets. Valuations typically run one to five times annual owner earnings, depending on size, risk, and transferability. That means more income per dollar invested. The trade-off is involvement. Business income often requires operational engagement, especially in the early years.

But here's the upside: businesses aren't limited by units. You can expand services, geography, or volume within the same entity. You don't have to buy another asset to grow. You scale the one you have.

This path rewards speed, intensity, and leadership. It punishes indecision and exposes weak operators fast. Cash flow forgives nothing. It tells the truth every month.

The Real Estate Machine

I controlled a few properties near Fort Bragg and rented them to Special Operations personnel coming in for extended training. The demand was predictable. Training cycles ran year-round. The stays were longer than typical short-term rentals, which meant less turnover and more stable income. I knew the market because I'd lived it. That knowledge gave me control most investors wouldn't have.

Real estate machines include long-term rentals, short-term rentals, commercial properties, and value-add plays like BRRRR. (Buy, Rehab, Rent, Refinance, Repeat). The key distinction: these are rental properties that produce ongoing cash flow. Flipping houses is active income. You work, you get paid once, you start over. That's Stage 3 income. Rental real estate pays you monthly whether you show up or not. That's Stage 4.

These assets offer leverage, appreciation, tax benefits, and cash flow. They benefit from natural, recurring demand. People need places to live, store, and operate. That demand exists before you show up, which creates downside protection while you learn.

Real estate is valued using cap rates, typically six to nine percent. That means every dollar of net operating income supports roughly eleven to sixteen dollars of asset value. This is why real estate often appears to build net worth faster on paper, even when cash flow is identical to a business. The valuation framework itself amplifies balance sheet growth.

The trade-off is scale. Real estate revenue is limited by the number of units. To grow, you must acquire more assets. That takes capital, deal flow, and management infrastructure. But it also means each asset runs somewhat independently. One property underperforming doesn't sink the whole portfolio.

This path rewards patience, compounding, and stability. It punishes laziness disguised as passivity. Passive investors confuse delegation with abdication. Operators don't. Real estate is often a more forgiving first machine. The system absorbs more mistakes. But remember Chapter 14: risk is a function of knowledge and control. If you know a business deeply, that might be your better path.

The Hybrid Machine

Hybrid machines combine business operations with underlying real estate: self-storage, car washes, laundromats, assisted living facilities. You'll see Paul's story in Chapter 19.

These assets trade at higher cap rates than more passive real estate because they require systems, active management, and operational skill. In exchange, they offer business-level cash flow layered on top of real estate-backed value. You get both engines working at once.

This path rewards systems thinking and operational depth. Mistakes here are expensive. Mastery here is rare. The margin for sloppiness is zero. But for those who build the skill, hybrids can be the fastest path to freedom. They combine the income velocity of business with the wealth stability of real estate.

The Freedom Asset Test

Before you choose a machine, you need a way to evaluate it.

Most people buy investments with no framework. They follow trends or emotions. That's how Workers end up owning things that look responsible but don't actually move them toward freedom.

A true Freedom Asset must pass all six tests. If it fails one, it's not a machine. It's a distraction. And distractions are how ambitious people stay broke while feeling productive.

From here on, you don't get to call something an opportunity unless it passes this test.

1. Cash Flow: A Freedom Asset must pay you consistently. Not someday. Not just when you sell. Real freedom comes from income that shows up every month and reduces your dependence on a paycheck. Appreciation is a bonus. Cash flow is the requirement. This is what separates the top-right quadrant of the Freedom Matrix from everything else.

2. Control: You must be able to influence the outcome. If your returns depend entirely on decisions made by other people, you don't own an asset. You own exposure. A Freedom Asset allows you to adjust pricing, expenses, operations, or strategy to improve results. This is Driver 4: Operational Performance. Control is what turns effort into leverage.

3. Leverage: A Freedom Asset allows you to use other people's money. This doesn't mean reckless debt. It means intelligent structure. The ability to control a large income-producing asset with a relatively small amount of your own capital dramatically accelerates wealth-building. This is one of the clearest separators between Owners and Workers.

4. Value Creation: You must be able to improve it. If the only way an asset grows is by waiting, it's fragile. A Freedom Asset allows you to add value through better management, systems, marketing, or operations. Your knowledge and effort should directly increase income and equity. This is forced appreciation through Driver 4.

5. Tax Efficiency: A Freedom Asset works with the tax code, not against it. The tax system rewards owners, operators, and builders. Assets that allow depreciation, deductions, or preferential tax treatment compound faster because less money leaks out to taxes every year. What you keep matters more than what you make.

6. Inflation Resistance: A Freedom Asset holds up when money weakens. Assets that produce income from real demand like housing, services, storage, and utilities tend to adjust with inflation over time. When prices rise, income rises with them. That protects your purchasing power instead of eroding it. This is Driver 1 working in your favor.

The Rule

If an opportunity doesn't pass all six tests, it's not a Freedom Asset. It might be a trade. It might be a hobby. It might even be profitable. But it won't predictably set you free.

When I evaluated my own path, I ran every opportunity through this filter. The ones that passed became the foundation of my portfolio. The ones that failed, no matter how exciting they seemed, got cut. The Amazon store I mentioned earlier? It failed the Control test. I learned that lesson the expensive way.

How These Paths Differ

Every deal is different. The same asset class can produce wildly different results depending on structure, terms, market, and operator. But a few patterns are worth understanding before you choose.

Speed to Income Replacement

Businesses can often replace earned income faster. If you earn $100,000 at a job, it's possible to acquire a simple business producing similar owner earnings and step into income replacement relatively quickly. Doing the same through real estate usually requires more scale, more time, or more capital.

The trade-off is responsibility. Business income often comes with operational involvement, especially in the early year or two. Speed and responsibility rise together. There's no free lunch. Only conscious trade-offs.

Financing Follows Structure, Not Category

Many people assume financing options are dictated by asset class. That's rarely true.

Seller financing, SBA loans, private capital, and creative structures exist across both real estate and business acquisitions. Outcomes are shaped by what you buy and how you structure it, not by whether it's labeled real estate or business.

Fit Matters More Than Fashion

No universally best path exists. There is only the path that aligns with your skills, your capital, your appetite for responsibility, and what you're optimizing for at this stage of life. Speed. Stability. Control. Scale.

The mistake is not choosing the wrong asset. The mistake is choosing a path that doesn't match who you are and then wondering why it feels heavy.

Owners don't follow trends. They follow fit.

What This Means for You

Both paths can lead to freedom. Business machines often move faster but demand more involvement. Real estate machines often compound slower but forgive more mistakes. Hybrids blend both.

The next few chapters will show you what each looks like in practice, starting with business acquisition in Chapter 18, then real estate in Chapters 19 and 20.

Pick the machine that fits. Then build it.

CHAPTER 18

Business as a Freedom Asset: Buy It or Build It

Jeremy worked as a home inspector earning $68,000 a year. Same inspections, same customers, same skills. Half of every dollar went to the owner.

Then the owner decided to retire.

Jeremy bought the business for $150,000. Zero money down. Five-year term. He didn't change jobs. He changed sides of the equation.

Five years later, the business crosses seven figures in revenue. Jeremy clears $175,000 in owner profit and doesn't need to perform inspections himself unless he wants to.

Same skills. Same market. Completely different outcome.

That's the power of owning the machine instead of working inside it.

Most people think entrepreneurship means negative cash flow, a shrinking bank account, and explaining to your family why you're working twice as hard for half the certainty. That picture keeps millions permanently employed.

But Jeremy didn't start from zero. He bought a machine that already worked.

Two paths lead to owning a business machine. You can buy one that already works. Or you can build one from scratch while your job covers the bills.

Acquisition is faster but requires capital or creative financing. Starting from scratch is leaner but requires skill, patience, and runway. Both lead to the same destination: ownership.

This chapter covers both.

The Acquisition Path

Every year, tens of thousands of profitable small businesses quietly change hands. Owners age out, burn out, or want liquidity.

Most owners are operators, not empire builders. They created a good job for themselves where they had control. Eventually, they want to retire, slow down, or move on. When that happens, the business doesn't disappear. It gets sold.

That creates an opportunity most people never see because they're too busy thinking entrepreneurship must start at zero.

When you acquire a business, you're not buying a job. You're buying cash flow, customers, systems, brand presence, operating history, and a platform you can improve. You're buying a machine.

A job pays you if you show up. A machine pays you because it exists.

Early on, acquisition often looks like Stage 3 income. You're involved. You work. You earn based on results. But unlike a job, this stage evolves.

With ownership and control, your Stage 3 effort compounds into Stage 4 or Stage 5 income. Systems replace labor. Teams replace your hours. Eventually, the machine produces income whether you show up or not.

That's Driver 4 in action. Your effort directly increases income and equity. You're not waiting on the market. You're forcing appreciation through operational improvement.

How Jeremy's Deal Worked

Let me show you the numbers behind Jeremy's story. He was one of two inspectors at the company. Each inspection cost $525. Jeremy kept half of each one he completed. He averaged about 260 inspections per year, earning roughly $68,000 annually. Solid Stage 3 income but capped by his time.

The company grossed about $325,000 the prior year. Jeremy personally generated roughly $135,000 of that revenue. After paying Jeremy his $68,000, the remaining income covered overhead and still left meaningful profit for the owner.

The purchase price was $150,000. That included the brand, customer pipeline, website, scheduling systems, a vehicle, and all equipment. Roughly 1.3 times owner earnings.

Jeremy financed the entire purchase. Zero money down. Five-year term. Monthly payment: about $3,375.

He walked into ownership without writing a check.

Nothing about Jeremy changed. Same skills. Same inspections. Same customers calling the same phone number. But now, instead of keeping half the dollars, he kept all of them. And he could scale.

A few months in, Jeremy added a third inspector. Soon after, he began training a fourth. The production from additional inspectors covered overhead and the loan payment. Every inspection Jeremy personally completed now went straight into his pocket at the full rate.

With four inspectors doing similar volume, the business generates over $500,000 in revenue. After paying inspectors, overhead, and debt service, Jeremy clears roughly $135,000 in owner profit, plus whatever inspections he personally chooses to do.

Once the loan was paid off, his income jumped another $40,000 per year.

He owns the machine.

Run It Through the Filter

Jeremy's deal passed every test in the Freedom Asset framework:

Cash flow from day one. Customers already existed. Revenue was proven.

Control over the outcome. Jeremy could hire, train, expand territory, raise prices, and improve systems.

Leverage through financing. Zero down. Debt service covered by operations.

Value creation through his own effort. Every improvement he made increased income and equity.

Tax efficiency through business ownership. Depreciation on equipment, deductible expenses, and business structure advantages.

Inflation resistance through service-based demand. People always need home inspections. When prices rise, inspection fees rise with them.

Six for six. That's why it worked.

The Build Path

Acquisition isn't the only way.

If you have a marketable skill and know demand exists, you can build the machine from scratch. The trade-off is time instead of capital.

My wife launched a service company with $2,000. Within a year, she was netting $4,000 to $5,000 per month. No acquisition. No loan. Just skill, hustle, and a willingness to figure it out.

The key is keeping your job while you build. Your paycheck covers the bills. Your side hours build the machine. You're not betting everything on an unproven idea. You're validating demand with real customers while you still have income security.

Once the business produces enough to replace your paycheck, you make the leap. Not before.

This path takes longer. But it requires almost no capital, builds skills through direct experience, and lets you prove the model before you depend on it.

You Don't Have to Be the Technician

The biggest mental block people have is thinking they have to be the expert.

You don't.

Most successful buyers are not the best technician. They're the owner. They learn how the machine works, then build systems and teams to replace themselves. A buddy of mine did this with an accounting firm. He's not an accountant, but he's expanding their services.

You're not buying your way into more work. You're buying your way into control.

This Is Not a One-Off

Jeremy's story is not rare. It's a pattern.

You see this same structure in painting companies, HVAC, plumbing services, pool cleaning routes, landscaping companies, pest control businesses, laundromats, car washes, digital agencies, and dozens of other service businesses.

These businesses are not flashy. That's why they work. They solve necessary problems. They have recurring demand. They produce real cash flow. And many are owned by operators who want out.

The model is always the same: buy or build cash flow, replace yourself over time, turn effort into ownership, turn ownership into freedom.

The industry barely matters. The structure always does.

The Real Point

Jeremy didn't invent anything new. He didn't gamble. He didn't quit without a plan.

He bought a machine that already worked.

My wife didn't wait for the perfect opportunity. She started with what she had while her income was covered.

Both paths lead to the same place: ownership of a machine that produces income whether you show up or not.

Stop assuming freedom must be built from zero. Stop renting your time inside someone else's system. Own the machine. Let effort compound into equity, income, and control.

The path is not rare. It's simply invisible to people who never learned to look for it.

The next chapter shifts to real estate and shows you why it remains the foundation of more millionaires than any other vehicle.

CHAPTER 19

Real Estate as a Freedom Asset

My personal money machine is built on real estate. Not because I love self-storage, houses, or apartment buildings, but because it works. It's consistent. Scalable. Repeatable. And it aligns with the Freedom Asset Test better than almost anything else with a strong mix of cash flow and appreciation.

Real estate isn't about drywall. It's about control, cash flow, and time. It's one of the cleanest Stage 4 systems out there: do the work once, get paid for years.

I didn't chase get-rich-quick. I built get-free-for-sure by staying in the top-right quadrant of the Freedom Matrix. By applying the principles in this book, I stacked Freedom Assets one deal at a time. The result is financial independence, seven-figure equity, and income that no longer depends on my time. All within a few focused years.

Think back to your hometown. Who was the wealthiest person you knew? Odds are, they owned a business or they owned real estate. Probably both. That's not a coincidence.

A Note on Categories

I've owned a mix of real estate assets. Apartment buildings and short-term rentals that ran with relatively little involvement once stabilized. And self-storage, which looks like real estate but operates more like a business.

Some of what I'll cover in this chapter falls into the hybrid category from Chapter 17. The real estate is the foundation, but you're running a business on top of it. Daily operations, customer acquisition, staffing, pricing. That's what makes models like storage, car washes, laundromats, and assisted living facilities hybrid.

I'm covering them here because the underlying asset is still real estate. The land, the buildings, the leverage, the tax treatment, the equity. What matters is that the structure passes the Freedom Asset Test and moves you toward Stage 4 or Stage 5 income.

Why Real Estate Works

You already know the Freedom Asset Test from Chapter 17. Real estate passes it cleanly.

It produces cash flow while you own it, not just when you sell. It allows leverage, so you control large assets with relatively small amounts of your own capital. It rewards control, because your decisions directly influence income and value. It benefits from durable demand, since people always need places to live, work, and store things. It compounds tax-efficiently through depreciation, deductions, and legal deferral strategies. And equity becomes fuel, not a trap, because you can access it without selling the asset.

That's why it's the backbone of so many fortunes.

Core Real Estate

My apartment buildings and short-term rentals are closer to pure Stage 4 income. Once stabilized, they produce consistent cash flow with relatively light operational involvement. The asset does the work. I manage, I optimize, I make decisions. But I'm not running daily business operations.

For most people, this is the clearest path to real estate wealth. Buy right, stabilize, manage well, and let the asset compound over time. It's not passive, but it's not a job either. It's ownership.

Hybrid: My Self-Storage Business

Self-storage looks like real estate but operates like a business. That's why it's hybrid.

I didn't go looking for a storage facility. One found me. A local broker mentioned a property he was listing. Physically, it looked fine. Financially, it was a disaster. Gross revenue was around $3,300 per month and expenses exceeded income. Roughly 140 units were occupied, but only about 40 tenants were actually paying. The owner had neglected operations entirely.

At the time, I had no background in self-storage. But the math was straightforward. Demand existed. Operations were broken. That gap was the opportunity.

The purchase price was around $2,000,000. I negotiated a structure with roughly 15 percent down. The seller financed the remaining balance at a below-market interest rate with 9 months before any principal or interest payments were due. That gave us time to stabilize the asset before debt service kicked in.

My total cash out of pocket was $10,000 in earnest money, which was returned at closing. We raised $300,000 for the down payment and closing costs, structured the seller note, and took control without using a bank.

There was work to do. We cleaned up units, fixed billing, enforced leases, adjusted pricing, and rebuilt systems. We spent nights and weekends out there while still working full-time. It was real work.

But the value created from that effort was massive. That's how you collapse timelines. Not by waiting for appreciation. By forcing it through focused action.

Today, that property generates about $38,000 per month in gross income. Expenses run under 20 percent. Even after refinancing, it produces five figures per month in net cash flow.

A few years after purchase, the property appraised for roughly $5.5 million.

Approximately $300,000 of raised capital turned into about $3.8 million in equity and a five-figure monthly income stream within a few focused years.

That outcome didn't come from market timing or luck. It came from control. We increased income, which increased value. That's Driver 4. Forced appreciation instead of waiting for it.

The Common Thread

Core real estate, hybrid models, hybrid strategy. The labels matter less than the structure.

In every case, the real estate foundation provides leverage, tax efficiency, equity growth, and downside protection. What varies is the level of operational involvement and where the primary income comes from.

Pick the model that fits your skills, your capital, and your appetite for responsibility. But understand that real estate, in some form, is the foundation under most lasting wealth.

Next Steps

You don't need millions to start. You don't need a perfect market. You don't even need to be an expert.

You just need one small move that nearly eliminates your biggest expense, puts you on the ownership side of the equation, and builds equity from day one.

It's called the house hack.

CHAPTER 20

House Hack Your Way to Freedom

Paul and his wife wanted to open a strength and conditioning gym. Most people in that position lease space and hope the business can out-earn the rent. Paul took a different approach.

They bought a warehouse building with two units. One side was already leased to a brewery, a sticky tenant with heavy buildout costs and no reason to move. That tenant covered nearly 90 percent of the mortgage from day one. The other unit became their gym.

Their largest expense, rent, was almost completely eliminated before they ever opened the doors. The business didn't need explosive growth just to survive. It only needed to be good.

Paul combined business and real estate into one move. He owned the building. He ran the business. His tenant paid his mortgage. That's the hybrid strategy from the last two chapters working together.

But you don't need a commercial building or a business to run this play. The same principle works with a duplex and a job.

What Is House Hacking

House hacking is simple. You buy a property, live in part of it, and rent out the rest. The rental income covers most or all of your mortgage. In some cases, it puts money in your pocket every month.

You can do this with a single-family home by renting out spare bedrooms. But the most powerful version is a small multifamily property: a duplex, triplex, or fourplex. You live in one unit and rent the others. When structured right, your tenants cover your entire housing cost.

You're not just saving money. You're building equity, generating income, and learning the fundamentals of real estate with training wheels on. This is Stage 4 wealth-building disguised as a housing decision.

Who This Is For

Let me be direct. House hacking isn't for everyone.

If you have a family of four, you're probably not moving into a duplex so strangers can live on the other side of the wall. That's fine. This strategy isn't aimed at you.

But if you're younger, single, recently married, or simply flexible, house hacking is one of the most effective wealth-building moves available. It's almost unfair how well it works for people willing to make one strategic sacrifice early.

The Financing Is Easier Than You Think

Most people assume they need a massive down payment to buy real estate. They're wrong.

If you're a veteran, your VA loan lets you buy with zero down payment and no private mortgage insurance. If you're a civilian, an FHA loan lets you get in with just 3.5 percent down. In rural areas, USDA loans may also offer zero down.

That's the bank putting up 96.5 to 100 percent of the money. You bring the plan and the commitment. They bring the capital.

This is leverage working in your favor from day one.

The Numbers in Action

On a fourplex around $500,000, FHA puts you in for about $17,500. Rents from the other three units nearly cover the mortgage. With VA or USDA, they can eliminate it entirely.

Either way, your biggest expense disappears while your tenants build your equity. Even if you're short a few hundred dollars a month at first, that's still a radically different game than paying full rent. And rents don't stay flat forever. Your principal and interest mostly stays fixed.

You benefit from appreciation. You get tax deductions. And your income grows as rents increase every year.

This isn't theoretical. House hacking is how Maria changed her financial trajectory. She ran the numbers on a duplex near her work. Two units. She lives in one, rents the other. Her housing cost dropped to $200 a month. For the first time in her adult life, her paycheck isn't disappearing into someone else's equity.

That's when the mindset shifts from saving to building.

The Snowball Effect

House hacking is a launchpad, not a destination.

One small multifamily deal can eliminate your housing cost, build equity, and generate cash flow all at once. That single move can permanently change your financial trajectory.

The real power shows up when you repeat it. Every two to four years, you move into the next property and run the same play again. By the fifth move, it's realistic to own a small portfolio that replaces a solid salary. No boss. No stock market dependence. No eighty-hour weeks.

Now stack discipline on top. While you live rent-free or nearly free, pay yourself phantom rent. Take the $1,500 to $2,000 you would have spent on housing and set it aside. After two years, you've quietly built the down payment and reserves for the next deal using money you were already conditioned to spend.

Momentum becomes exponential. Start earlier, and the snowball has more time to roll.

BRRRR: Recycling Capital to Scale

House hacking gets you started. BRRRR is how you accelerate.

Buy. Renovate. Rent. Refinance. Repeat.

You buy a property below market value, improve it, stabilize it with tenants, refinance to pull your capital back out, and repeat the process with the same dollars.

The renovate step doesn't mean gutting the property. It could mean paint, minor repairs, or nothing at all if the deal is already undervalued. The principle is capital efficiency, not construction. You're buying right, improving where it makes sense, and recycling your investment to keep scaling.

Here's how house hacking and BRRRR combine. You house hack your first property. Live in one unit, rent the others, eliminate your housing cost. Over a year or two, you stabilize it, build equity, and learn the fundamentals. Then you refinance, pull out some or all of your original capital, move into your next house hack, and repeat.

Each cycle builds equity, cash flow, and experience. Each property becomes a machine that keeps producing whether you're there or not.

This isn't get-rich-quick. It's get-free-for-sure. Slow, deliberate, and relentless.

A Note on Flipping

Flipping is a legitimate business model. Done well, it can produce strong income. But by default, flipping is Stage 3 income. You get paid when the deal closes. When the project ends, the income stops.

If you like the mechanics of flipping, finding undervalued properties, solving problems, forcing appreciation, BRRRR is how that skill turns into ownership instead of just income. You do the work, but you keep the asset. The machine stays.

This Isn't Forever

Most people eventually want a single-family home with a yard and no tenants next door. Great. That's allowed.

But doing one or two strategic multi-unit moves first puts you miles ahead of your peers for the rest of your life. You're not choosing between lifestyle and wealth. You're sequencing them correctly.

Parents, this applies to your kids too. Instead of paying for dorms or apartments they'll never own, help them buy a small property near campus. They live in one unit, rent the rest, and graduate with equity, cash flow, and a real asset instead of a diploma and debt. That's a life-altering head start.

This isn't about living like a monk. It's about being strategic once or twice so you don't have to struggle forever.

My Regret Becomes Your Advantage

If I could go back in time, this is the single move I would have made first. I started later. I learned the hard way. I missed years of cash flow, equity, and tax benefits.

But you don't have to.

The thing holding most people back isn't money. It's fear. But once you take action, fear evaporates. It gets replaced by momentum, ownership, and confidence.

One house hack can change your entire financial life. In real cash. In real equity. In real freedom.

Start Here, But Think Bigger

House hacking and BRRRR are great entry points. They're accessible, repeatable, and effective.

But if you want to build real wealth faster, you'll eventually need to scale beyond that first deal. Bigger properties. Bigger upside. Bigger leverage. Bigger cash flow.

That's where we're headed next.

CHAPTER 21

The Case for Going Bigger

Most people start building wealth because they want out of the grind. Then they accidentally build themselves a new one. They trade one boss for ten little jobs. One ceiling for another.

They own assets, but the assets own their time. Not because ownership is a trap, but because they never built the support around it. No manager. No bookkeeper. No systems. They kept every task because it felt like control.

And when it gets heavy, they call it "safer" to stay small. Then they wonder why freedom is taking so long.

Starting small teaches you the game. Staying small traps you in it.

Scale is what turns effort into engines, jobs into systems, and income into independence. In real estate, that means moving past single-family houses into multifamily, self-storage, mobile home parks, and other commercial assets. In business, it means moving past side hustles into real operating companies that produce cash flow, can be improved, and can be leveraged.

Different vehicles. Same physics of freedom.

You don't start here. You grow into it. But this is where the math finally works in your favor.

Economies of Scale

Buying ten single-family homes means ten roofs, ten HVAC systems, ten insurance policies, ten tax bills, and ten separate locations. Ten small problems instead of one efficient system.

Buy a ten-unit apartment building and suddenly it's one roof, one insurance policy, one tax bill, one operating platform. Same number of units. Completely different level of efficiency.

The same logic applies in business. You can run ten tiny operations, each with their own rent, software, insurance, and management headaches. Or you can scale one core platform and let size do the work for you.

Most of the expensive pieces don't grow in a straight line with revenue. The building, systems, leadership, and back office stay relatively fixed while sales and customers multiply on top. Each additional dollar of revenue drops onto an already-built foundation. Margins expand. Cash flow accelerates.

That's what scale changes. Not just income. Efficiency and control too.

Andre Built an Empire One Van at a Time

A friend of mine, Andre, started as a licensed electrician working for someone else. Good at the trade. Reliable. But tired of making money for the owner while his own ceiling stayed fixed.

He launched his own company with one van and a phone number. Did the work himself. Grew his reputation. Within a couple years, he had three vans on the road and crews running jobs without him.

That was growth. But Andre wanted scale.

Two of his competitors were older guys looking to exit. Tired of the grind. No plan for what came next. Andre approached them separately and bought both companies.

Before the acquisitions, Andre had overhead: office space, insurance, dispatch software, marketing, bookkeeping. Each competitor had the same costs. Three companies, three sets of expenses.

After consolidation, Andre had one office, one dispatcher, one insurance policy, one marketing budget, and one bookkeeping system. But now he had the combined revenue of all three companies flowing through that single infrastructure.

Duplicate costs disappeared. Margins expanded. Market share grew. He went from competing with those companies to absorbing their customers and crews into his own system.

Today Andre runs the operation. He rarely touches a screwdriver. He's not the technician anymore. He's the owner of a machine that produces cash flow whether he shows up or not.

That's the difference between growing and scaling. Growth adds revenue. Scale adds leverage.

You Control the Value

You've seen this math before. Now watch what happens when you add zeros.

In commercial real estate and business, value is driven by income. Grow revenue. Tighten operations. Expand margins. Value follows.

Buy a service business earning $200,000 a year at a 3x multiple. You pay $600,000. Improve operations and grow earnings to $300,000. At the same multiple, the business is now worth $900,000. You created $300,000 in value by increasing cash flow.

Real estate works the same way.

You buy a 10-unit apartment building. Each unit rents for $1,000 a month. After expenses, the property produces $60,000 in net operating income.

Raise rents by $100 per unit. That's $12,000 a year in additional net income.

At a 7 percent cap rate, that one move creates $171,000 in new value.

Scale that across 100 units and you've added over $1.7 million in value. Same action. Same math. Just more zeros.

That's Driver 4 at scale. Workers wait for markets to go up. Owners make their own numbers go up.

Better Financing and More Negotiation Power

Small assets are financed like consumer purchases. Big assets are financed like businesses.

When you buy a single-family home, the bank underwrites you. Your W-2, your credit score, your debt-to-income ratio.

When you buy a commercial property or operating business, the bank underwrites the asset. Its income. Its stability. Its ability to service debt. If the deal produces cash flow, it qualifies.

Larger assets also unlock flexibility: interest-only periods, longer amortizations, non-recourse loans, and seller financing. Business owners and commercial property owners think in cash flow and exit strategy, not just price. That creates room for creative structures that don't exist in consumer real estate.

Partnerships Unlock Scale

Scale also opens the door to partnerships that small deals can't support.

If you have time but not capital, you can find a partner with money who doesn't want to operate. If you have capital but not time, you can find a partner who will do the execution.

A $50,000 single-family rental doesn't leave room for two people. A $2 million apartment building or a business acquisition does. The economics justify splitting the load and the upside.

Rachel bought her first car wash three years ago. Did the work herself at first, learned the equipment, optimized the membership model. Now it runs without her daily involvement and throws off solid cash flow.

She found a second location. Great area, motivated seller, good numbers. But she was tapped out on capital.

Vanessa is a corporate attorney. High income, no time, no expertise in operations. She wanted her first deal to be with someone who already knew what they were doing.

They partnered up. Rachel brought the deal, expertise, and operations. Vanessa brought the capital. Rachel's management fee is built into expenses. Vanessa gets a preferred return on her capital. After that, they split remaining cash flow 65/35.

Rachel knows 35% of a second car wash is better than 100% of nothing. Vanessa knows her return is lower than doing it herself, but she'd never do it herself. Two years later, they're looking at a third location.

People without money get into bigger deals this way. And how people without time get into deals at all.

Scale Buys Back Your Time

When you first get started, you do everything. You're the salesperson, operator, bookkeeper, and the one who gets the call when something breaks at 11 p.m.

That's normal at the beginning. But staying small means staying trapped in the parts you hate.

Scale is how you buy your time back. The manager, the bookkeeper, the systems you avoided hiring? They're not overhead. They're freedom.

Andre started by answering every call and running every estimate. Now he has a dispatcher, an office manager, and crew leads who handle day-to-day. He focuses on growth, deals, and strategy.

Scale lets you offload what you hate, double down on what you're good at, and move into the only role that creates freedom: owner of the machine, not the one stuck inside it.

Built to Survive Downturns

When the economy tightens, people don't stop needing housing, storage, repairs, or basic services. They downshift. They rent instead of buy. They consolidate. Demand shifts toward exactly the assets that produce steady cash flow.

Andre's business grew during the last downturn. People weren't buying new houses, but they still needed electrical repairs, panel upgrades, and code compliance. Essential services don't disappear when the economy contracts. They concentrate.

And when the economy expands, these assets grow with it. Rents rise. Service demand increases. Pricing power returns. The same assets that held steady in the downturn accelerate in the upturn.

Freedom Assets aren't built on optimism. They're built on necessity. That's why they survive when others collapse and compound when others recover.

Start Then Scale

Starting small is fine. It's how most people enter the game. One rental. One small business. One acquisition that teaches you how cash flow and ownership actually work.

That stage matters. You build reps. You make mistakes on a scale you can survive.

But if you stop there, you hit a ceiling. Adding one unit or one client at a time keeps you trapped as the technician instead of the owner. Busy but not free.

The people who build real freedom don't scale effort. They scale the system.

Start where you are. Learn the game. Build confidence. But don't confuse small and safe with smart. At some point, staying small isn't caution. It's fear dressed up as wisdom.

What Comes Next

Now that you've seen what real assets and real ownership can do, it's time to confront the strategy most people are told is the smart path to wealth.

Because compared to building and owning cash-flowing, controllable assets, the stock market story the middle class has been sold starts to look very different.

Let's settle that next.

CHAPTER 22

Stocks Versus Freedom Assets: The Showdown

Index Funds Have Outperformed Other US Assets Over Time

The Results of a $100 Investment in 1970

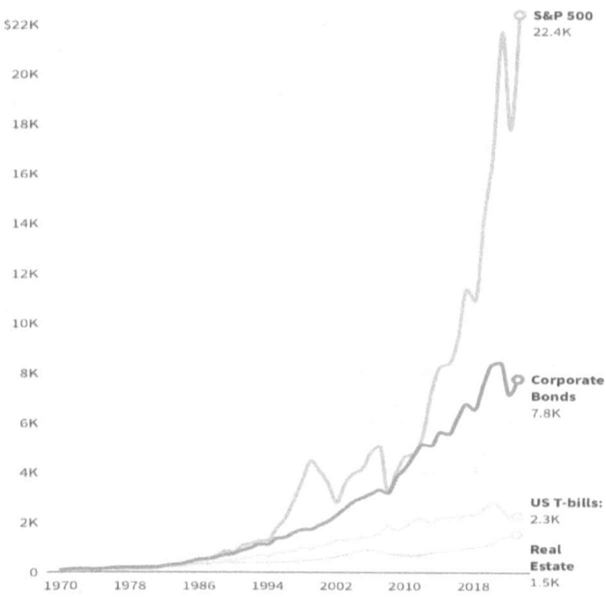

The above uses NYU Stern School of Business data to compare the growth of $100 invested in the S&P 500 (returns include dividends), Baa corporate bonds, three-month U.S. T-bills, and real estate as calculated through the Case-Shiller Home Price Index.

Chart: Investopedia/Peter Gratton • Source: New York University Stern School of Business

Investopedia

You've probably seen a chart similar to this. It probably says something similar to this, "Just invest in the S&P and you'll be a millionaire." It's clean. Visually impressive. Comforting. And completely misleading.

We've heard it a hundred times from financial advisors and retirement planners: "Just invest in the S&P 500 and hold for the long term. It's the proven path to wealth." And to back it up, they flash a chart like this one.

If you make financial decisions based on charts like this, you'll spend decades stuck in the slow lane investing in the Speculative Wealth quadrant while the wealthy build real, scalable freedom through Freedom Assets you're told to ignore.

How They Rig the Data

According to the chart, one hundred dollars invested in the S&P 500 in 1970 grows to $22,400 by 2022, while real estate only grows to $1,500.

Case closed, right? Wrong.

In Special Forces we're taught to question the intel, not just accept it. Most investors never do that. They take what's fed to them and move out. I pulled that chart straight from Investopedia's "The 10 Rules of Investing: The Simple Path to Wealth." It isn't just misleading. It's engineered to sell you a product and keep you playing their game.

I picked up that magazine in an airport bookstore while researching this book, curious what kind of advice the average investor was being spoon-fed. It took me one minute to find this chart. But what you're really seeing is a masterclass in data manipulation. A case study in how to lie without technically lying.

That chart is the reason millions of Americans will work 40 years and still retire scared.

Just look at it: the S&P 500 curve rockets up while real estate limps along at the bottom. To the casual reader, it's an open-and-shut case. Why would anyone touch real estate?

But did you read the fine print? Let's unpack it.

Myth #1: The Time Horizon Is Unrealistic

This chart covers 52 years, from 1970 to 2022. That's great for theoretical modeling, but it doesn't reflect real life.

It assumes you start investing at 15 and never touch your money until you're 67. No pauses. No drawdowns. No life interruptions.

And no recessions. Like the 12-year stretch between 1996 and 2008 when the S&P 500 basically returned 0%. If you planned to retire around 2008-2010, you felt the pain of that one. You lost a whole decade of returns the system promises.

They're asking you to wait 52 years for a chart that looks good on paper but ignores real life.

Myth #2: They Use the Weakest Real Estate Metric Possible

The "real estate" line on the chart is based on the Case-Shiller Home Price Index, which only tracks resale prices of single-family homes. It doesn't measure real estate as a total investment. It only shows appreciation.

Let's break it down:

- That $100 turning into $1,500? That's a 1,400% total return over 52 years.
- Compare it to the S&P's $22,400 return: a 22,300% gain.
- The compound annual growth rate for real estate is 5.35%. For the S&P, it's 10.97%.

Seems like stocks win. But wait. They stripped out everything that makes real estate powerful: cash flow, tax benefits, leverage, and control. Then they called it a fair comparison.

They assume every house is bought in cash and never rented out. When is the last time you or anyone you know bought an investment property in cash, then let it sit without ever renting it?

Real estate investors use financing. They put 10-30% down and borrow the rest. That one factor alone blows the doors off the 5.35% number.

Meanwhile, the chart includes reinvested dividends for the S&P 500 to boost that return. So it strips away what makes real estate powerful but includes what boosts stocks. Convenient.

Myth #3: They Rig the Visual

Check out the vertical axis on the chart. It stretches long while keeping the horizontal axis short, making the S&P line shoot almost vertically by the end. This exaggerates the gap visually.

It's a tactic straight from the classic book "How to Lie with Statistics" by Darrell Huff: stretch the vertical scale, compress the horizontal scale, remove context, choose incomplete data, package it with a shiny headline.

It's not about showing the truth. It's about making the S&P look unstoppable and real estate look like a waste of time.

Myth #4: They Show Compound Growth for Stocks, but Not for Real Estate

The reason the S&P 500 looks so dominant is because they reinvested dividends. Real estate? They assume you never reinvest a single dollar of cash flow, never refinance, never add value, never scale. One asset compounds while the other gets frozen in time.

To be fair, real estate cash flows, leverage, and tax benefits are hard to quantify in a broad chart. Cash flow varies by property, market, management, and financing terms.

But that's exactly why real estate works: you have control over those variables. You can increase cash flow, improve operations, and optimize for tax savings. You can compound through action, not passive hope.

The S&P? You get what you get. If you want more, you wait longer or put more money in.

You've been fed half the truth, packaged to sell you on a passive plan that keeps your money locked up for decades.

Whenever anyone challenges me on this, their argument is always the same: Freedom Assets aren't passive, but stocks are. My answer is always the same too: not really. Retirement accounts aren't truly passive either. That 10% you're saving is 10% of your time. On a 40-hour week, that's four hours. You're already spending it – just to lock money away for decades and hand 20% or more to the government on the way out. I'd rather spend those same four hours buying and building Freedom Assets that pay me now and forever, protect my principal, and don't get taxed like ordinary income in my golden years.

How People Actually Invest

When I compare leveraged real estate to unleveraged stocks in the case study that follows, I'm comparing how these assets actually get used by real people. Here's why.

Most people don't even know leveraging stocks is possible. No HR benefits meeting covers it. No financial advisor recommends it to the average retirement investor. The entire system is designed around cash contributions and patience.

And for most retirement investors, leverage isn't even an option. Traditional 401(k)s, IRAs, and Roth IRAs prohibit margin trading by regulation. The vast majority of Americans invest through these accounts. Leverage was never on the table.

Even outside retirement accounts, almost no one does it. Only about 10% of retail investors use margin. The standard advice is to dollar-cost average into index funds with cash from your paycheck. That's how the system is designed. That's how almost everyone uses it.

Real estate is the opposite. Almost everyone finances. A 20% down payment with an 80% loan isn't aggressive. It's the default. Banks expect it. The system is built for it.

There's a reason leverage is common in real estate but rare in stocks: control.

Leverage without control is gambling. When you buy stocks on margin, you're betting on outcomes you can't influence. You don't control the company. You can't improve its operations. You can't force its value up. A margin call can wipe you out based on decisions made in a boardroom you'll never see.

That's why margin trading is reserved for professionals who live and breathe the markets. Not for the teacher investing for retirement. Not for the fireman stacking a nest egg. Not for anyone reading this book.

Real estate leverage is different. You control the asset. You can raise rents, cut expenses, add value. The leverage is tied to something you can operate. That's Driver 4. And that's why this comparison reflects reality, not theory.

The Case Study

What follows is a detailed case study. I'm going deep here because this is the comparison most people get wrong. Follow the math. Check my numbers. Then decide for yourself.

Stocks use long-term historical average returns with dividends reinvested. Real estate uses conservative assumptions on appreciation, rent growth, and expenses, with no value-add, aggressive leverage, or creative financing. This isn't a best-case scenario. It's a conservative one.

The Stock Investor's Case

Let's say you've got $50,000 to invest. You follow the herd and park it in the S&P 500 like all the "experts" tell you to and wait.

- Initial Investment: $50,000
- Historical Average Return: 10% (including dividend reinvestment)

The Future Value Formula

$FV = PV \times (1 + r)^n$

- FV = Future Value (what it grows to)
- PV = Present Value (what you start with)
- r = Rate of Return (your annual percentage gain)
- n = Number of years Compounding

$FV = \$50{,}000 \times (1.10)^{10} = \$129{,}687.12$

That means $50,000 growing at 10% per year for 10 years becomes $129,687.

But let's pause. That $50,000 sat in an account for a decade. You're staring at numbers on a screen. Nothing changes. No cash. No control. No ability to add value. Just hope. Hope that the market doesn't crash right before you need it. Hope that inflation doesn't erode your gains. Hope that nothing in your life forces you to pull it out early.

Now, let's put that same $50,000 into rental real estate.

The Real Estate Investor's Case

Same $50,000. Different approach.

- You use it as a 25% down payment on a $200,000 rental property.
- The bank finances the remaining $150,000 at 7% interest on a 30-year mortgage.
- You rent it out for $1,900/month. Tenants cover the mortgage while you build wealth.

Let's talk through all the factors and numbers so you can understand everything. Then I'll compare them side by side with stocks in a chart so it's easier to follow.

1. Leverage

With $50,000, you control a $200,000 asset. That's 4x leverage, a $150,000 boost to your wealth-building machine. Your tenants are paying down the loan for you while you gain income, appreciation, and equity.

2. Cash Flow (Monthly Income)

Let's calculate the income after expenses:

- Gross Rent: $1,900/month ($22,800/year)
    - Increases 2% per year (compounds)
    - Conservative 5% vacancy
    - Total Rental Income Collected:
        - Over 10 Years: $237,000
        - Over 20 Years: $526,000
- Mortgage Payment:
    - $997.95/month ($11,975/ year) at 7% for 30 years
    - Payment does not change.
- Property Taxes, Insurance & Maintenance: $460/ month ($5,520/ year)
    - Increases 3% per year (compounds)
    - US Averages for $200,000 home
        - Insurance - $1,800
        - Property Tax - 0.90%
        - Maintenance - about 1%
    - Total Expenses Paid

        - Over 10 Years: $63,281
        - Over 20 Years: $148,324

- Net Cash Flow (Profit): Net cash flow is what's left after rent, operating expenses, and the mortgage are paid. This is real money you can use today, not paper gains.
    - Year 1 Calculation:
        - $22,800 in scheduled rent

          - $1,140 in vacancy (5%)

          - $5,520 in operating expenses

          <u>- $11,975 in mortgage payments</u>

          = $4,165 in annual net cash flow
    - That's approximately $347 per month in income.
    - Total Net Cash Flow Collected:
        - Over 10 years - $54,136
        - Over 20 Years - $138,448

These figures assume a 5% normalized vacancy rate, no rent shocks, and no value-add improvements. This is conservative underwriting designed to reflect real ownership, not a best-case scenario. To see the breakdown of all the math, see Appendix 2.

3. Loan Paydown (Building Equity)

Each mortgage payment reduces your loan balance, automatically growing your equity. Original loan amount: $150,000.

- Annual mortgage payment: ~$11,975
- In the first 10 years, roughly 15% of the original loan balance is paid down.
    - Approximate principal paid in first 10 years: ~$21,000–$23,000
- After 20 years, roughly 40–45% of the loan balance has been paid down.

  - Approximate principal paid after 20 years: ~$60,000–$70,000

You didn't write a check for that equity. Your tenants did. This is an invisible return most investors never count.

4. Appreciation (Increasing Value)

Real estate has historically appreciated at 4–6% per year over long periods. To stay conservative, we'll use 4%.

On a $200,000 property:

- Year-one appreciation:

  $200,000 × 4% = $8,000

- Over time, appreciation compounds:

  Value = $200,000 × 1.04

Because you only invested $50,000, that $8,000 gain represents a 16% return on your invested equity in year one purely from appreciation.

That leverage effect continues every year:

- The property appreciates on the full $200,000 value
- You benefit from that growth with only $50,000 invested

Over time:

- 10 years: $96,048 in appreciation
- 20 years: $238,224 in appreciation

The appreciation rate stays the same, but the dollar gains grow larger each year because the appreciation is applied to a higher asset value. Since you control that asset with a smaller amount of invested capital, leverage magnifies the return on your equity over time.

5. Tax Benefits (Keeping More of Your Money)

Real estate investors legally pay less in taxes through deductions and depreciation.

- Common write-offs include mortgage interest, property taxes, insurance, maintenance, management, and operating expenses.

- Depreciation allows you to deduct the value of the building over time, even while the property itself may be appreciating.
    - Residential rental property is depreciated over 27.5 years
    - Typically, 70–80% of the purchase price is allocated to the structure (the rest is land and not depreciable)

For a $200,000 rental:

- Depreciable basis (75% estimate): $150,000
- Annual depreciation deduction: ~$5,455/year

At a moderate tax rate (22–32%), that depreciation alone can translate into:

- $1,500-$2,500 per year in tax savings

Over time:

- 10 years: ~$15,000-$25,000
- 20 years: ~$30,000-$50,000

These savings come from income you already earned, money you keep instead of sending to the IRS.

Return After 1 Year

	Stocks (S&P)	Real Estate
Initial Investment	$50,000	$50,000
Cash Flow Profit	$0	$4,165
Loan Paydown	$0	$1,500
Appreciation Profit	$5,000	$8,000
Tax Benefit Profit	$0	$2,000
Total Profit	$5,000	$15,665
Total ROI	10%	31%

Total Returns After 10 Years

	Stocks (S&P)	Real Estate
Initial Investment	$50,000	$50,000
Cash Flow Profit	$0	$54,136
Loan Paydown	$0	$21,281
Appreciation Profit	$79,687	$96,048
Tax Benefit Profit	$0	$20,000
Total Profit	$79,687	$191,465
Total ROI	159%	383%

Here's what it looks like at 20 years.

20-Year Comparison

	Stocks (S&P)	Real Estate
Initial Investment	$50,000	$50,000
Net Cash Flow	$0	$138,448
Loan Paydown	$0	$64,050
Appreciation Profit	$286,375	$238,224
Tax Benefit Profit	$0	$40,000
Total Profit	$286,375	$480,722
Total ROI	573%	961%

Ten years from now, while your friend brags about their $130,000 index fund, you're pulling in monthly income, watching tenants pay down your loans, and holding a $200,000+ net profit from one single deal. Or twenty years from now with a $480,000 profit that you didn't just watch happen. You built it.

Why Freedom Assets Win

Factor	Stocks	Real Estate
Source of Returns	Price appreciation, dividends	Cash flow, appreciation, loan paydown, tax benefits
Leverage	None	Control a $200,000 asset with $50,000
Tax Efficiency	None – Capital Gains Taxes	Depreciation, write-offs, 1031 Exchanges
Risk Mitigation	None – Market swings, emotional	Insurability, tangible, always in demand
Control	None – controlled by news cycles, corporations, and algorithms	You control rents, expenses, and value-adds

Stocks Can't Keep Up

Stocks fail the Freedom Asset Test. No cash flow. No control. No leverage. No tax efficiency.

The example we just ran used real estate because the math is easy to show. But the same principles apply to business. Cash flow. Control. Leverage. Tax advantages. The ability to force value through your own effort. That's what separates Freedom Assets from passive speculation.

The case study didn't even include value-add improvements like renovations, rent increases, or operational plays that can supercharge returns. That's the real power of Freedom Assets: you can force appreciation and manufacture wealth with strategy, knowledge, and effort.

That's how you can become financially free in 3-10 years versus waiting and sacrificing 30-40 years using your IRA and 401(k) as your plan for freedom.

The Real Risks of Freedom Assets

Freedom Assets aren't risk-free, but the risks are often misunderstood.

In real estate, the biggest risk is liquidity. You can't click a button and sell tomorrow. It takes time, buyers, and the right market conditions. In business, the risks include customer concentration, operational complexity, and cash flow timing.

But most risks are self-induced. Bad analysis. Over-leveraging. No reserves. That's not the asset. That's poor execution.

Even good operators get caught in downturns. But as we covered earlier, the operators who survive are the ones who stress-tested before they bought, kept reserves, and never let one bad quarter force a sale.

The risks are real. They're also manageable for anyone willing to do the work before signing.

Should You Avoid Stocks Completely?

Not necessarily.

If your employer offers a 401(k) match, take it. That match is free money giving you an instant 100% return on your contribution. You'd be crazy to leave that on the table.

Just don't confuse that with a wealth-building strategy. A 401(k) match is a tactical move. It's not a plan for financial freedom.

The Bottom Line

Wall Street was built for hedge funds, insiders, and institutions. Your money is the liquidity they feed on. They profit on volatility while you ride the rollercoaster and hope.

Freedom Assets flip the script. The game doesn't go to the fastest algorithm. It goes to the person who understands how to find opportunity, manage risk, and create value.

Would you rather keep betting your future on a system you don't control that was never built for you? Or would you rather build a portfolio of cash-flowing assets you control, that meet basic human needs, that pay you every month regardless of what the Fed or Wall Street decides?

Financial freedom isn't found in charts, speculation, or hope. It's found in ownership. Control. Cash flow.

Freedom Assets beat stocks because they multiply your wealth through multiple streams of return. But now, what if you could take all those streams and make them compound?

In the next chapter, I'll show you how to turn one deal into many.

CHAPTER 23

Compound It

After my first deal, I stopped.

Not on purpose. Life just got busy. Work picked up. Family needed attention. The deal was cash-flowing. I told myself I'd get back to it when things calmed down.

Two years passed. I didn't buy anything. I didn't grow. I let my reasons become my excuses.

Looking back, I wasn't busy. I was comfortable. That first deal gave me just enough progress to feel like I was on the path. But I wasn't building. I was coasting. And coasting doesn't buy freedom.

Most people do the same thing. One deal, maybe two, then nothing. They keep working their job, hoping that maybe, 30 years from now, they'll be free.

This chapter is about not making that mistake. Or if you already have, about starting again.

If you're still reading this, you probably don't want to wait 30 years. You want financial freedom. The kind where you walk away from your job because you choose to. The kind where your investments pay you more than your paycheck. Where time is yours again.

Maybe your vision goes deeper. Maybe you're building a legacy. Generational wealth. Assets that feed your kids and grandkids in an uncertain future. Something that lives on after you.

That doesn't happen by accident. And it doesn't happen by buying and holding one or two properties or running one small business forever. If you want wealth that grows with momentum and compounds year after year, you need to leverage what you've already built and use it to acquire more income-producing assets.

This is the Value Loop in action. Income increases value. Value creates equity. Equity funds acquisition. Acquisition creates new income. Each asset spins up the next.

Remember when I told you equity sitting in your home is dead equity? The same is true with your rental portfolio or your business. Untapped equity and uninvested profits don't pay the bills. They don't grow your cash flow. They just sit there, silent and unused.

The wealthy know how to put that capital to work. That's what this chapter is about: turning equity and profits into a weapon to win the war for financial freedom. Turning one deal into many. Managing your equity to scale your asset base, which gives you options later that most people never have.

How to Compound: Real Estate

When you build equity in a property, either through time or by forcing appreciation, you have two choices: let it sit there with an ROI of 0%, or put it to work to acquire more assets.

Most people do the first. Or worse, they push to pay off their rental early. This kills growth.

Wealth builders do the second. Just remember the golden rule: only compound when the math is undeniably in your favor.

Here are the best strategies to extract and deploy equity into your next cash-flowing asset:

1. Cross-Collateralization: Use the equity in one property as the down payment and collateral on another without bringing new cash to the table. The lender records both properties as collateral and covers the down payment on your new purchase.

This keeps your capital free for other opportunities while allowing you to expand faster. The downside is it ties multiple properties to one loan. If you default or want to sell one, the lender controls them all. Powerful leverage, but it costs you flexibility.

2. Cash-Out Refinance: Refinance an existing property for a higher loan amount, pull out the difference in cash, and use it to acquire another asset. You get liquidity without selling, your equity keeps compounding, and your cash goes back to work.

Example: You owe $200,000 on a property worth $400,000. You refinance at 75% LTV and pull out $100,000 cash. That's a full down payment for your next deal.

The cash you pull out is tax-free because it's debt, not income. The key is to never pull more equity than the new asset can comfortably cover. If the new property easily pays the added debt service, the move is smart. If it doesn't, don't do the deal.

3. HELOC: A Home Equity Line of Credit works similarly to a cash-out refinance, but gives you access to a revolving credit line instead of a lump sum. You can use it to fund a down payment, renovations, or float deal costs, then pay it back as cash flow comes in.

The Principle Is the Same

All these tools do one thing: they turn dead equity into productive capital.

The question you need to answer first: will the new debt payment on the extracted equity be easily outweighed by the income it generates in the new asset?

If your new asset cash flows $1,000/month and the debt service on the equity you pulled is $500/month, you just created $500/month in net income. Borrow at 6%, put it to work making 9%+. That's how you beat the banks at their own game.

How to Compound: Business

The same principle applies to business, just with different mechanics.

When your business generates profit beyond what you need to operate, you have the same two choices: let it sit idle or put it to work.

Business owners compound in three ways:

1. Reinvest in Growth

Plow profits back into the business. New equipment. More marketing. Additional staff. Expanded territory. Each dollar reinvested should generate more than a dollar in future returns.

2. Acquire Competitors

Remember Andre from Chapter 21? He didn't just grow his electrical company organically. He bought two competitors. Their revenue stacked onto his infrastructure. Duplicate costs disappeared. Margins expanded. He went from competing with those companies to absorbing their customers and crews into his own system.

That's compounding through acquisition. Instead of building market share one customer at a time, you buy it in chunks. Each acquisition adds income while the shared infrastructure multiplies efficiency.

But here's what most people miss. As Andre's company grew, he stopped being the technician. He built systems. Hired managers. Removed himself from daily operations. The business became less dependent on him.

That shift doesn't just free up his time. It changes the value of the business. It feels counterintuitive, but the less Andre's business needed him, the more it became worth. A business that depends on the owner is just a job. A business that runs without the owner is a sellable asset.

A small owner-operated company might sell for 1-2x earnings. A larger, systematized company with management in place can command 3-5x earnings. Scale even larger with professional management, documented processes, and predictable revenue, and private equity firms start paying attention at 6x, 8x, or higher. The same business, built differently, can be worth five times more. The ceiling keeps rising the more you remove yourself and systematize.

The more efficient the business becomes and the less it relies on the owner, the higher that revenue compounds into value.

Andre's reinvestment didn't just grow his income. It expanded his multiple. The Value Loop compounds both cash flow and the value of the entire enterprise. That's how business owners build real wealth, not just a job they own.

3. Roll Profits into Other Freedom Assets

Many business owners take a portion of their profits and invest in other Freedom Assets. Some acquire additional businesses. Others buy real estate.

Reinvesting in another business can generate faster returns, but requires more involvement. Real estate is typically slower but provides better equity growth over time, equity that's easier to leverage into more acquisitions. Real estate also tends to be more passive once stabilized, allowing your wealth to compound with less ongoing effort.

Real estate often becomes the long-term foundation. Business generates active income. Real estate builds durable wealth underneath it. Over time, the real estate portfolio grows into an easier legacy asset, something you can pass on without requiring the next generation to operate a business.

The wealthy don't choose one or the other. They do both. Business profits fund real estate acquisitions. Real estate equity funds business expansion. The Value Loop spins across asset classes.

Case Study: How We Bought an $8,500,000 Storage Facility Without Using Our Own Money

Let me show you exactly how my partners and I used cash-out refinance to buy a storage facility without putting up a single dollar of our own cash.

Step 1: The Existing Property

We owned a self-storage facility that had appreciated significantly, quadrupling in value, because we increased rents and occupancy, the market improved, and we optimized operations.

Step 2: The Opportunity

I found another storage facility for sale that was cash-flowing with massive value-add potential. I negotiated the purchase price to $7,000,000.

Step 3: Structuring the Deal

Instead of using our own money for the down payment, we approached the bank with a proposal to use equity from an existing property as the down payment for an acquisition of another property. The bank appraised our original property and determined we had enough equity to cover the $1,750,000 down payment needed while staying under their loan-to-value requirement.

They refinanced our original property, pulled out the $1,750,000, and structured a new $5,250,000 loan for the purchase.

Step 4: The Outcome

We acquired a $7,000,000 asset with zero money out of pocket. The new property immediately cash flowed, covering the loan and putting more money in our pockets. The initial appraisal came in at $8,500,000, giving us $1,500,000 in equity on day one. As we implemented value-add strategies, the new property appreciated by 40%, creating even more equity for the next deal.

1031 Exchange: Trade Up Without Paying Taxes

Cross-collateralization and refinances are how you scale without pulling cash from your own pocket. The 1031 exchange is how you scale into bigger assets without paying taxes.

A 1031 exchange allows you to sell an investment property and reinvest 100% of the proceeds into a bigger property without triggering capital gains taxes. Technically, you're deferring taxes, not avoiding them. But you can keep deferring for life and pass them to your heirs tax-free. That means you compound your equity and grow your wealth tax-free for decades.

1031 in Action

You bought a rental for $200,000 ten years ago. It appreciates to $400,000. You've paid down the loan and now have $290,000 in equity. Normally, you'd owe about $40,000 in capital gains taxes.

Instead, you roll that full $290,000 into a new $800,000 asset using a 1031 exchange. You now own an 8-12 unit apartment building instead of one house. 4x the appreciation potential, more cash flow, zero tax bill.

Do that every few years. Your equity compounds. Your cash flow grows. Your tax bill stays zero. You can't do that with a 401(k).

Equity Is Fuel

Most people treat their assets like savings accounts. They buy one property or build one business, let the equity sit there, and wait 30 years. That's wasting potential.

The second mistake is paying off debt early or hoarding cash in a business account. It feels safe. But it kills compounding. The safest place for capital is inside more cash-flowing Freedom Assets, not trapped inside a paid-off property or sitting idle in a bank account earning almost nothing.

Smart investors and operators activate their equity and profits. They put capital back to work. One property becomes two. One business funds another. Two become four. Four become an empire. Equity stops being static and becomes kinetic. Money in motion creates more money.

Staying small is a choice. So is scaling. Neither is wrong. But if your goal is freedom, understand that freedom requires a certain scale. You don't have to build an empire. But you do have to build enough that your assets replace your income. Stopping short of that isn't safety. It's choosing a slower, harder path.

And if you decide later in life that you want to simplify? Scaling gives you that option too. If you've built a portfolio of ten apartment complexes, you can sell six and use the proceeds to pay off the other four. Now you have 40% of the operational load but similar net cash flow. No debt. Less complexity. Same income. You couldn't do that if you'd stayed small. The person with two paid-off duplexes doesn't have that flexibility. Scaling first, then deleveraging later, gives you choices. You can stay aggressive or downshift into simplicity. The point is you get to decide. Different paths for different seasons of life.

That's the difference between "having a rental" or "owning a business" and building financial freedom. Between waiting 30 years and changing your life in 3-10 years.

Your equity isn't a trophy. Your profits aren't meant to sit idle. They're fuel. They're supposed to move, multiply, and buy back your time, your options, and your independence.

CHAPTER 24

Building True Legacy Wealth

Sydney was four years old the first time she walked a property with us. Nora was two, riding on my hip, taking it all in without understanding a word. My wife had been managing this property while I was deployed. She handled the tenants, the maintenance calls, the decisions. Now we were walking it together as a family.

Sydney asked questions. She watched how we talked to the property manager. She saw us check the units, look at the numbers, make decisions together.

She won't remember the details. But she'll remember that her parents owned things. That we built something together. That wealth wasn't something we hoped for. It was something we created.

That moment changed how I think about everything we're building. It's not just about escaping the grind anymore. It's about what we leave behind.

The Shift from Freedom to Legacy

When you first start building wealth, it's about buying back your time. Making work optional. But once you taste that freedom, a new question emerges:

What legacy will I leave behind? Who else can I lift up? What kind of life can I build for my family, not just now, but long after I'm gone?

And legacy doesn't require children. It can mean lifting siblings, parents, partners, communities, or simply ensuring you never pass financial fear forward. Legacy is responsibility extended beyond yourself.

Legacy isn't just about passing down money. It's about passing down a system. A mindset. A model for freedom that your family, kids, grandkids, and great-grandkids can use to build wealth for themselves.

The ultra-wealthy operate this way. Families like the Rockefellers didn't just accumulate assets. They passed down knowledge. They built frameworks to preserve and grow wealth across generations.

Meanwhile, most people spend their lives working, saving, and eventually spending down those savings just to survive. Their wealth dies with them.

That doesn't have to be you.

Think about the endgame of the Accumulation Trap.

You save for 40 years. You retire with a decent nest egg. Then you slowly spend it down. As you age, medical bills start to grow. Long-term care costs $8,000 to $15,000 a month, draining the nest egg you spent your entire working life building. Your savings shrink. The stress grows. Eventually, you may need to sell the house just to pay for hospice. If the money runs out before you do, you become a financial burden on your children, the people you spent your whole life trying to provide for. You die with little to nothing left. Your kids inherit whatever remains, if anything.

That's the reward for doing everything "right."

I know this sounds pessimistic. But it's real. It happens every day to good people who followed the rules.

Freedom Assets change that math. The assets produce income. That income pays for your life and your care. You never have to sell. You never drain the principal. You never become a financial burden to your children. When you're gone, your kids inherit the machine still running, still producing, still compounding.

Freedom Assets as Legacy Assets

Whether it's real estate, a business, or a hybrid of the two, the principles are the same. What matters is that you own something that produces income, appreciates over time, and can be passed forward.

Real estate pays you forever through rental income your family can count on. It multiplies itself as one property funds the next. It protects against inflation as rents and values rise. And it teaches ownership through tangible assets your kids can learn to manage.

Business delivers the same benefits. A well-run company throws off income, teaches leadership, and gives your family a living system they can improve. It can scale quickly, and the more it systematizes, the more it's worth. Whether it's a service business, a construction company, or a storage facility, the key is the same: own it, grow it, pass it on. Your kids can inherit the customer base, the systems, and the momentum you built.

My wife built her own business while raising our daughters. Sydney and Nora will grow up watching both their parents build, not just earn. That's the model we're passing down.

The vehicle matters less than the principle. Build something worth inheriting. Then teach them how to own it.

Assets Without Knowledge Are a Liability

Here's a sobering stat: 70% of wealthy families lose it all by the second generation, 90% by the third.

Not because they lacked effort or intelligence, but because the money was passed down without the systems and mindset that created it.

Money without wisdom is a liability. Legacy wealth isn't just about what you leave behind. It's about what you pass forward. That means teaching your kids how to buy assets instead of liabilities, use good debt to build cash flow, leverage tax advantages, and grow wealth through control rather than compliance.

If your kids are young, let them come with you to meetings. Bring them to work in the business. Walk your properties with them. Show them how your machine works. Then, when you're both ready, hand them the keys.

That's how you raise builders, not just beneficiaries.

Getting Your Spouse on Board

Most couples aren't misaligned on values. They're misaligned on timing and risk. One person sees the current path isn't working. The other sees change as dangerous. That tension is normal, especially when money and family are involved.

The mistake most people make is trying to win the argument instead of reducing the risk. You don't need your spouse to fully believe in the vision on day one. You need them to feel safe enough to take the first step.

That means learning more and maybe starting smaller than you want to. Smaller than the plan in your head. Small enough that failure wouldn't damage trust or stability. One deal. One asset. One controlled move. When the downside is limited and the upside is real, fear loses power. Results do what arguments can't.

I've seen this over and over. The moment an asset produces actual income, not projections, the conversation changes. Not because someone was persuaded, but because reality showed up and the fear of the unknown dissipated. Alignment rarely comes before action. It usually follows proof.

Leadership here doesn't mean dragging your spouse forward or dismissing their concerns. It means taking responsibility for learning, structuring, and protecting the downside so they don't have to carry that weight.

Over time, the questions change. Not "Is this safe?" but "What's next?" That's how real partnerships are built. Not through pressure. Through competence and follow-through.

If you're building freedom for your family, your first job isn't persuasion. It's stewardship. Protect the downside. Prove the model. Let trust compound the same way the assets do.

You're the Fork in the Family Tree

If you grew up in a family that struggled financially, welcome to the club. Most of us did, not necessarily through any fault of our parents. But someone has to break that cycle. Someone has to be the first to change everything.

Why not you?

What if your kids didn't have to worry about college debt? What if they started adulthood owning cash-flowing property or equity in a family business? What if your grandkids didn't even know what "living paycheck to paycheck" felt like?

That future is possible. But only if someone in the family decides to play a different game. Only if someone rewrites the rules. Only if someone builds the foundation for the generations that follow.

That someone is you.

Let Them Dream Bigger

Most parents teach their kids to dream "realistically." It's not cruelty. It's caution. They've felt the stress. They've been burned by the system. They want their kids to be "safe." So, they nudge them toward stability. A steady job. A sensible career. Something secure.

But security without freedom is just a comfortable cage. A lion in a zoo is more secure than one in the wild. But which one is actually alive?

What if your kids never had to choose between passion and practicality? What if money wasn't the limiting factor in their decisions but a tool they already knew how to create?

What if they could say yes to the things that light them up, whether that's travel, music, art, or service, without asking "Can I afford this?" Because the assets you built already pay the bills.

That's the kind of freedom real wealth creates. Not just financial freedom, but option freedom. The freedom to chase meaning, not just survival.

And that starts with you. Not by handing them a free ride, but by showing them the road. By giving them the tools. By teaching them how the machine works so they can drive it even further than you did.

Legacy Starts Now

Most people think legacy is about what happens after you die. They're wrong.

Legacy starts now. Every asset you buy instead of every liability you consume. Every conversation with your kids about money and mindset. Every action you take toward freedom.

You're not just investing in assets. You're investing in possibilities. You're building the world they will inherit and the lens through which they will see everything.

You Just Saw What's Possible

This chapter wasn't meant to give you more tactics. You've already got those. It was meant to lift your eyes. To help you see what's really at stake.

This isn't just about money. This is about generational transformation. About being the one who breaks the cycle and builds a new standard.

You've seen what's possible. You've seen how a single decision, done right, can echo for decades.

But vision without action is just a daydream. You've got the blueprint. You've seen the map.

The next step isn't about making money. It's about rewriting your family's story.

Let's talk about what comes next.

CONCLUSION

The Choice

If you've made it this far, something is already different. You don't just know more about money. You see it differently.

You understand why the traditional path feels so tight even when you're doing well. You can see the trade most people never notice: trading time, energy, and options for the illusion of security.

That awareness separates you from the crowd. But awareness isn't the goal. Freedom is.

Freedom doesn't arrive all at once. It's built deliberately, decision by decision. And you now understand something most people never do.

Financial freedom isn't an age. It isn't a number in an account. It's an income structure built on ownership, leverage, and control.

The Five Stages of Income aren't theory. They're a map. The Freedom Matrix isn't philosophy. It's a diagnostic tool.

You can now look at any job, any business, or any investment and ask the questions that actually matter:

1. Does this increase my control or reduce it?
2. Does this compound my effort or consume it?
3. Does this move me closer to owning my time or reinforce dependence?

Once you see the system this way, you can't unsee it.

No one is coming to give you permission. Not your employer. Not the government. Not the financial industry.

Freedom is something you build or something you delay. And delaying always feels reasonable in the moment. Another year. Another promotion. Another "when things settle down."

They never do.

But here's the good news. You don't need to overhaul your life overnight. You don't need millions. You don't need reckless risks.

You need to start directing your effort differently.

Acquire assets instead of accumulating promises. Buy back small pieces of your time and let momentum do its work.

One Freedom Asset changes how you breathe. Two change how you plan. Five change how you live.

This isn't get rich quick. This is get free for sure.

The system isn't going to change for you. It doesn't need to. It already rewards ownership, leverage, and initiative. Once you understand that, you can use it instead of fighting it.

The path is there. The map is in your hands.

I think about Sydney and Nora. I think about the life my wife and I are building together. Not just the assets, but what those assets mean: time with my family, options for my kids, a legacy that doesn't end with me.

That's why I wrote this book. Not as one path among many, but as the only path I've found that consistently and predictably creates financial freedom for a normal person on a 5-10 year timeline that doesn't consume your prime years.

What happens next is simple.

You decide whether to stay a Worker, trading your life for permission and hoping the pile gets big enough someday, or become an Owner, building something that pays you back in time, choice, and control.

Workers hope. Owners build.

Every worker is just a soldier. I was one too. You might be one right now. But your mission changes the moment you decide to stop executing someone else's plan and start building your own. The next twelve months will pass whether you act or not. The only question is which side of the Freedom Matrix your actions will feed.

Are you saving like a Worker, or building like an Owner?

Your move.

Go Here Next

Get Your Book Bonuses

If you haven't yet, get your book bonuses to get started. I have given you a ton of free, useful resources to accompany this book and help you take action on everything you've learned.

Go to: **SterlingSeizert.com/BookBonuses**

Or scan the QR code:

And Join the Buy Your Freedom Community

If this book opened your eyes to what's possible, the next step is to put it into action. Doing it alone is really hard. Instead, do it alongside hundreds of people who are doing the same.

The Buy Your Freedom: Unconventional Wealth Community on Skool is where we go deeper. It's where financial freedom stops being theory and becomes your reality.

Inside, you'll get access to:

- Ongoing training and case studies
- Live mentorship and Q&A
- A network of people building wealth the same way you are

This is where you turn knowledge into action and action into freedom. Join the community. Build your freedom. Scan the QR Code or check out: www.skool.com/buy-your-freedom

Scan Me

For Military & Veterans: Join the War Room

When I started buying real estate, I didn't go it alone. I had a community of military investors who'd already done it.

That's what **The War Room Mastermind** by From Military to Millionaire gave me, and what it can give you. Inside, you'll find:

- Active-duty and veteran real estate investors
- Real deal analysis and accountability
- Access to likeminded mentors who've walked the path

This is where real military members and veterans collaborate, close deals, and build wealth.

Scan the QR code or visit: https://www.frommilitarytomillionaire.com/buy-your-freedom

APPENDIX 1

Start Here: Choose your Path to Freedom

Let's be clear up front: you're not going to follow these roadmaps perfectly. And that's okay.

These are the big-picture paths and the strategic overview of how to go from where you are now to financial freedom. If you want video walkthroughs of each step, templates, and live coaching support as you follow your roadmap, grab the free Book Bonuses and join the Buy Your Freedom Skool community. That's where I help you implement everything in this book step by step, alongside other people walking the same path.

Some steps might take you longer than expected. Others might click into place faster than you thought. Life happens. You'll hit snags, speed up in some areas, and slow down in others. These roadmaps aren't meant as rigid checklists. They're guides meant to keep you from wandering aimlessly or second-guessing every decision.

Let this be your compass. I wrote these plans to be as clear, simple, and approachable as possible without overwhelming you. They're here to help you take action.

So take it step by step. If thinking about Phase 4 right now stresses you out, ignore it for now. It's just there to show you that a clear path exists, that there is another step after the one you're on, and that you won't be stuck in the beginning forever.

The timelines and asset types I mention are designed to feel within reach and to not overwhelm anyone. But don't feel boxed in by them. If you're ready to go bigger, go. If you're already experienced or have capital lined up, skip ahead. As you may recall, I didn't start small. I bought an 18-unit apartment building as one of my first major moves.

No one-size-fits-all strategy works for every person in every market. But these roadmaps will give you a structured, proven path–something to follow when the noise gets loud or when you feel stuck.

Pick the one that fits your current position. Read through the others. Adjust as needed. Revisit it often. But most of all, just start walking.

Roadmap #1: Zero to Freedom (Starting with Limited Capital)

This roadmap is for anyone starting with limited cash, maybe carrying debt, and stuck in the paycheck-to-paycheck cycle but ready to break out. This was exactly where I was when I started and where many of my students have started. Whether you're early to mid-career, still in college, in the military, or simply starting fresh, this plan gives you the exact steps to build real wealth through education, hustle, and smart acquisition of cash-flowing assets.

Your first major milestone: close on a 3–4 unit house hack and launch a side hustle by the end of Year 1. Again, if that doesn't interest you, skip ahead. This powerful combo sets you up to acquire a second asset in Year 2 and scale from there.

Phase 1: Mindset, Education & Foundation (Months 1–3)

Rewire your thinking. Get control of your finances. Start building the habits and knowledge base that will carry you forward.

- Weeks 1–2: Read or listen to one wealth-building book per week (on mindset, real estate, small business, leverage). Listen to daily podcasts to immerse your brain in new ideas.
- Weeks 3–4: Complete your personal financial statement: income, expenses, debts, assets, and net worth. Get clear on your current reality.
- Weeks 5–6: Identify and eliminate one "bad debt" or unnecessary expense. Redirect that money into savings. Begin monitoring and improving your credit score. You'll need it to qualify for financing.
- Weeks 7–8: Start paying yourself first, even just 1–5% of your income. This simple discipline is the foundation of your wealth engine.
- Weeks 9–12: Join 2–3 local or online investing communities (real estate, business, or wealth building). Start networking and absorbing the language of opportunity.
    - Join mine at www.skool.com/buy-your-freedom
    - If you're military or a veteran go here: https://www.frommilitarytomillionaire.com/buy-your-freedom

Phase 2: Capital Building, Income Growth & Deal Readiness (Months 4–9)

You need capital to invest, but you don't have to rely on savings alone. This doesn't have to be hundreds of thousands, just enough to cover some basics as you get going. Now's the time to grow your income, prepare for financing, and learn how to find a great deal.

- Month 4: Launch a side hustle that can bring in $500–$1,000/month. Choose something simple, skill-based, and scalable (see Chapter 12).

- Month 5–6: Optimize your side hustle: streamline the process, reduce time spent, and improve consistency. Set aside all earnings for investing.
- Month 7: Maximize your W-2 income. Ask for a raise, take on overtime, or shift to a higher-paying role. This boosts both your capital and your loan eligibility.
- Month 8: Start studying creative financing: seller financing, subject-to deals, lease options, and how to structure partnerships. Get comfortable thinking beyond "save for 20% down."
- Month 9: If business acquisition is your path, use Months 8-9 to study business brokers, learn to read profit & loss statements, and identify service businesses in your area doing $200K-$500K in revenue with owner-operators ready to exit.
- Month 9: If real estate is your path, learn how to analyze 3–4 unit multifamily deals. Run the numbers: rents, expenses, cash-on-cash return, debt coverage. Reach out to local lenders and mortgage brokers to explore FHA/VA options and get pre-qualified if possible.

Phase 3: Acquire Your First Freedom Asset (Months 10–18)

Time to take action. Your goal is to purchase a 3–4 unit property, live in one unit, and rent the others. This move eliminates (or drastically reduces) your housing expense while building equity and cash flow.

- Months 10–12: Analyze 5–10 deals per week. Drive neighborhoods. Talk to brokers and property managers. Learn your market inside and out.

- Months 13–15: Line up financing or partner capital. Make offers. Close on a 3–4 unit multifamily using FHA, VA, or a low-down-payment loan.
- Months 16–18: Move in, stabilize rents, and optimize the property. Reduce expenses. Improve tenant quality. Your housing cost just dropped; your net income just rose.

Phase 4: Expand & Acquire Your Second Freedom Asset (Months 19–24)

You've made the leap. Now it's time to scale. Your side hustle income, savings from reduced housing costs, and first asset cash flow all combine to fund your next move.

- Month 19–20: Tighten systems on your first property. Set up automated rent collection, maintenance processes, and tenant screening. You're not just a landlord. You're building a portfolio.
- Month 21–22: Decide on your next asset:
    - Another small multifamily
    - A self-storage facility
    - A cash-flowing small business (laundromat, cleaning service, vending, etc.)
    - Use creative financing or a capital partner if needed.
- Month 23–24: Acquire your second asset. Keep expenses low and reinvest all income into scaling your portfolio.

Phase 5: Scale, Reinvest & Build Legacy Wealth (Years 3–8)

By now, you've built habits, income streams, and confidence. Now it's time to go from tactical to strategic.

Year 3

- Scale to 5–10 units or $3K+/month in semi-passive income.
- Develop strong relationships with brokers, lenders, and capital partners.
- Start tracking your "Freedom Ratio": passive income ÷ monthly expenses.

Year 4

- Acquire a larger Freedom Asset (10–20 unit multifamily, 100+ unit storage facility, or a high-margin small business with a team).
- Consider joint ventures or syndications if you're ready to go bigger.

Year 5

- Hit "Survival Freedom": your Stage 4 and 5 income cover your basic lifestyle expenses.
- Choice: Reduce or leave your W-2 job only if passive income exceeds all expenses by 25+%, or continue to work to stack cash for more acquisitions.
- Begin optimizing taxes and asset protection strategies.

Years 6–8

- Target $5,000–$10,000+/month in recurring cash flow.
- Reinvest profits into more scalable assets.
- Begin long-term estate planning and intergenerational wealth transfers.

If you'd like to download this as a checklist with a video tutorial visit: www.sterlingseizert.com/roadmap1

Roadmap #2: W-2 to Freedom (For Higher-Income Earners Who Want Out)

This roadmap is built for professionals earning strong W-2 income but feeling stuck. You've done everything "right" (college, career, 401(k), maybe even home ownership), but you still feel like freedom is miles away. You make good money, but it all seems to disappear into taxes, bills, and lifestyle creep.

This plan is about redirecting your income into cash-flowing assets, using leverage wisely, building partnerships, and replacing your salary with true financial freedom, without starting from scratch.

Scan Me

skool.com/buy-your-freedom. If you want video breakdowns, analysis, and weekly support while following this roadmap, join the community.

Phase 1: Maximize & Redirect (Months 1–3)

You already earn good money. Now it's time to put that income to work.

- Weeks 1–2: Complete your personal financial statement. Audit your expenses for lifestyle inflation. Cut the fluff and reclaim your capital.
- Weeks 3–4: Maximize your W-2 income: negotiate a raise, bonus, or promotion. Even small increases compound when redirected into assets.
- Weeks 5–8: Redirect 10–25% of your income into a separate investment account. Automate it like a tax.
- Weeks 9–12: Start educating yourself. Read 1–2 books per month, listen to investing and entrepreneurship podcasts, and begin

networking with asset owners (real estate investors, small business operators, etc.). Figure out which asset type excites you most.

Phase 2: Build Your Asset Base (Months 4–12)

Now it's time to take your first swing. This phase is about action: putting capital into motion and gaining operational experience.

- Months 4–6: Analyze 50+ deals in your target asset class:
    - Small business (in industries where you have experience or strong operators)
    - Real estate (small multifamily, self-storage, mixed-use, etc.)
    - Other cash-flowing Freedom Assets (automated service businesses, mobile home parks, etc.)
- Months 7–9: Acquire your first Freedom Asset. Consider turnkey options or operating-light investments if your bandwidth is tight. The goal is cash flow and control, not speculation.
- Months 10–12: Optimize your asset: improve management, reduce expenses, and increase revenue. Document processes so you can scale.

Phase 3: Scale with Leverage (Months 13–24)

You've got proof of concept. Now use your capital, credibility, and relationships to go bigger.

- Months 13–15: Acquire a second Freedom Asset using conventional financing, saved capital, or a joint venture with family/friends. Think long-term scalability.
- Months 16–18: Build relationships with commercial lenders, private money partners, brokers, and operators. Expand your deal flow pipeline.

- Months 19–21: Refinance existing equity or use cross-collateralization to acquire your next property or business.
- Months 22–24: Systematize asset #1 and #2. Free up your time while increasing your cash-on-cash return. This is where the snowball starts to roll.

Phase 4: Portfolio Acceleration (Years 3–5)

The leap from hobby investor to professional wealth builder. Focus shifts from "owning more" to optimizing, scaling, and protecting.

Year 3

- Target value-add assets:
    - 10–20+ unit multifamily
    - 100+ unit storage facility
    - Operational small businesses with upside
- Use forced appreciation (renovations, better ops, revenue optimization) to increase net operating income (or EBITDA—earnings before interest, taxes, depreciation, and amortization), value, and cash flow.

Year 4

- Leverage your track record to raise private capital or partner on larger deals.
- Consider strategic partnerships, or maybe a syndication, if you want scale without doing it all yourself (I eventually did this too).
- Set target: $6,000–$10,000/month in recurring income.

Year 5

- Refine your portfolio: cut weak performers, double down on winners.

- Aim for $10,000–$15,000/month in passive or semi-passive income.
- Begin implementing advanced tax strategies: cost segregation, entity structuring, depreciation stacking.

Phase 5: Freedom & Legacy (Years 5–7)

You now own income-producing assets, not just a job. It's time to step into full control.

- When your income from assets exceeds your lifestyle expenses by 25-50%, consider exiting your current job W-2 world, or maybe scale your time back if you still enjoy it.
- Optimize portfolio for systems, tax efficiency, long-term appreciation, and stability.
- Create a comprehensive estate plan and implement asset protection strategies.
- Begin transferring wealth and wisdom to the next generation or start teaching others.

If you'd like to download this as a checklist with a video tutorial, visit: www.sterlingseizert.com/roadmap2

Roadmap #3: Late-Start Strategy Starting Your Wealth Journey in Your 40s or 50s

This roadmap is for those waking up to the fact that their current financial path won't cut it, not if they want real freedom before 65. Maybe you've been raising kids, building a career, or just didn't know any better until you read this book. But now you're ready to move fast, focused, and with urgency.

You may not have decades ahead to compound, but you do have wisdom, work ethic, and equity. This plan will show you how to use those advantages to build income, scale fast, and protect what you build.

Phase 1: Aggressive Repositioning (Months 1-6)

You don't have time to waste. This phase is about cutting fat, unlocking capital, and setting up the foundation to make your money move.

- Weeks 1–2: Complete your full financial inventory and personal financial statement. List all income, expenses, liabilities, and assets. Highlight anything that wouldn't be missed if liquidated or leveraged (home equity, unused vehicles, savings, retirement accounts, etc.).
- Weeks 3–4: Cut unneeded lifestyle expenses that won't be missed. Pay yourself first. Redirect that capital toward your new investment fund. This may include refinancing high-interest debt, downsizing, or adjusting discretionary spending.

Scan Me

skool.com/buy-your-freedom. If you want video breakdowns, analysis, and weekly support while following this roadmap, join the community.

- Weeks 5–6: Begin reading 1 book per month and listening to podcasts on wealth building, real estate, asset acquisition, and tax strategy. Education compresses timelines.
- Weeks 7–8: Only contribute up to employer match to tax-advantaged accounts (401(k), SEP IRA, HSA). Separate the rest for your capital fund for cash-flowing investments.

- Months 4–6: Join local investing groups or business owner meetups. Start building relationships with real estate brokers, property managers, commercial lenders, and small business operators.

Phase 2: High-Leverage Quick Wins (Months 7–18)

You don't need 20 doors; you need the right few Freedom Assets to move the needle. This is where you make your first strategic acquisition.

- Months 7–9: Seek small multifamily (5–10 units), short-term rental, self-storage (80-150 units), laundromat, or service-based businesses you understand.
- Months 10–12: Acquire your first income-producing asset using conventional financing, equity from an existing property, seller financing, or a capital partner. Set a floor: 10% cash-on-cash return minimum.
- Months 13–18: Improve your asset's performance. Force appreciation through renovations, rent increases, better management, or expense cuts. Document your systems and lessons learned, and prepare to scale.

Phase 3: Portfolio Construction (Months 19–24)

You've got proof of concept. Now it's time to multiply. You don't need 30 years of compounding; you just need a clear, high-yield, repeatable system.

- Month 19–20: Target your second and third acquisitions. Look for:
    - 8–12%+ cash-on-cash return
    - Value add potential

- Month 21–22: Use seller financing, 1031 exchanges, or partner capital to speed up acquisition without draining personal cash.
- Month 23–24: Aim to own 3–5 assets within 24 months. Focus on performance, not just volume.

Phase 4: Accelerated Scale (Years 3–5)

Now it's time to go from small wins to portfolio power. The moves here will determine if you reach full freedom or just coast toward retirement.

Year 3

- Use 1031 exchanges to upgrade into larger, more stable properties (10–30 units, commercial buildings, etc.).
- Begin tapping private lenders, retirement capital (SDIRAs—Self-Directed IRAs), or equity partners for larger deals.

Year 4

- Acquire a larger asset (self-storage facility, value-add multifamily, or a systematized business with staff).
- Consider strategic partnerships to extend your time, skills, and reach.
- Set target: $7,000–10,000/month in passive income.

Year 5

- Implement aggressive debt paydown on select high-interest or weaker assets.
- Aim for $10,000–$20,000/month in recurring income.
- Start transitioning out of active income (W-2 or business ops) if you haven't already.

Phase 5: Freedom & Protection (Years 5–7)

You've built momentum, income, and equity. Now it's time to solidify your freedom, protect your wealth, and plan your legacy.

- Optimize your portfolio for systems, tax efficiency, stability, and time freedom.
- Create a clear succession plan: Will your spouse, kids, or partners know how to run or sell your assets if something happens?
- Implement a comprehensive asset protection strategy using trusts, LLCs, and insurance.
- Structure everything for efficient wealth transfer to your heirs, while minimizing taxes and legal headaches.

Key Metrics to Track (For All Plans)

Monthly Metrics

- Total passive income
- Savings rate percentage
- Deals analyzed
- Network growth (new connections made)

Quarterly Metrics

- Net worth growth
- Equity position in all properties
- Cash-on-cash return for each investment
- Progress toward next property acquisition

Annual Metrics

- Total portfolio value
- Effective tax rate

- Freedom ratio (passive income ÷ expenses)
- Time spent managing investments

Success Principles for All Roadmaps

1. Consistency over intensity: Small daily actions compound more effectively than sporadic massive efforts. If you can be consistently intense, then great, but definitely make sure you're consistent.
2. Focus beats diversification: Master one strategy before expanding.
3. Speed through knowledge: Invest in education and mentorship to avoid costly mistakes.
4. Leverage OPM: Other People's Money accelerates your timeline.
5. Cash flow first, appreciation second: Never sacrifice income for theoretical future gains.
6. Systems create freedom: Document and systematize everything, from tenant screening to maintenance.
7. Control creates wealth: Maintain decision-making control in all investments.

Remember: Your timeline may vary based on local market conditions, starting capital, and execution. These roadmaps provide a framework, but your personal journey will require adjustments based on opportunities and challenges that arise along the way. The goal is progress, not perfection.

APPENDIX 2

20-Year Rental Property Cash Flow Breakdown

$200,000 Home | $50,000 Down | $150,000 Loan at 7% for 30 Years | $1,900/mo Starting Rent | 5% Vacancy | 2% Annual Rent Increase | 3% Annual Expense Increase

Year	Gross Rent	Vacancy (5%)	Net Rent Collected	Operating Expenses	Mortgage Payment	Annual Net Cash Flow	Cumulative Cash Flow
1	$22,800	$1,140	$21,660	$5,520	$11,975	$4,165	$4,165
2	$23,256	$1,163	$22,093	$5,686	$11,975	$4,432	$8,597
3	$23,721	$1,186	$22,535	$5,856	$11,975	$4,703	$13,300
4	$24,196	$1,210	$22,986	$6,032	$11,975	$4,978	$18,279
5	$24,679	$1,234	$23,445	$6,213	$11,975	$5,257	$23,536
6	$25,173	$1,259	$23,914	$6,399	$11,975	$5,540	$29,076
7	$25,677	$1,284	$24,393	$6,591	$11,975	$5,826	$34,902
8	$26,190	$1,310	$24,881	$6,789	$11,975	$6,116	$41,018
9	$26,714	$1,336	$25,378	$6,993	$11,975	$6,410	$47,428
10	$27,248	$1,362	$25,886	$7,202	$11,975	$6,708	$54,136
11	$27,793	$1,390	$26,403	$7,418	$11,975	$7,010	$61,145
12	$28,349	$1,417	$26,931	$7,641	$11,975	$7,315	$68,461
13	$28,916	$1,446	$27,470	$7,870	$11,975	$7,624	$76,085
14	$29,494	$1,475	$28,020	$8,106	$11,975	$7,938	$84,023
15	$30,084	$1,504	$28,580	$8,349	$11,975	$8,255	$92,278

Year	Gross Rent	Vacancy (5%)	Net Rent Collected	Operating Expenses	Mortgage Payment	Annual Net Cash Flow	Cumulative Cash Flow
16	$30,686	$1,534	$29,152	$8,600	$11,975	$8,576	$100,854
17	$31,300	$1,565	$29,735	$8,858	$11,975	$8,901	$109,755
18	$31,926	$1,596	$30,329	$9,124	$11,975	$9,230	$118,985
19	$32,564	$1,628	$30,936	$9,397	$11,975	$9,563	$128,548
20	$33,215	$1,661	$31,555	$9,679	$11,975	$9,900	$138,448
TOTAL	$553,980	$27,699	$526,281	$148,324	$239,509	$138,448	

Note: Year 10 and Year 20 rows are bolded for reference. Cumulative Cash Flow represents total net cash in your pocket after all expenses and mortgage payments. Mortgage payment is fixed for the life of the loan. Operating expenses increase 3% annually.

Endnotes

1. Social Security Administration. Retirement Benefits: Replacement Rates.
2. U.S. Bureau of Labor Statistics. National Compensation Survey.
3. Federal Reserve Board. Survey of Consumer Finances.
4. Employee Benefit Research Institute. Retirement Savings Adequacy Reports.
5. Social Security Administration. Actuarial Life Tables.
6. U.S. Department of State, Office of the Historian. Nixon and the End of the Bretton Woods System.
7. U.S. Bureau of Labor Statistics. Consumer Price Index for All Urban Consumers (CPI-U).
8. U.S. Bureau of Labor Statistics. CPI Inflation Calculator.
9. Federal Reserve. History of the Federal Reserve.
10. Federal Reserve Act, Section 2A.
11. Cantillon, Richard. Essay on the Nature of Trade in General. 1755.
12. Internal Revenue Service. Federal Income Tax Brackets.
13. Internal Revenue Service. Capital Gains Tax Rates.
14. Internal Revenue Service. Publication 946: How to Depreciate Property.
15. Internal Revenue Code §1031.
16. S&P Dow Jones Indices. Historical Returns Data.

17. Federal Reserve Bank of St. Louis. M2 Money Stock (M2SL).
18. SmartAsset. U.S. Retirement Savings Statistics.
19. American Council on Aging. Retirement Security and Economic Insecurity Studies.
20. Sowell, Thomas. Economic Facts and Fallacies. New York: Basic Books, 2008.
21. U.S. Department of Agriculture, Economic Research Service. Food Price Outlook. Bureau of Labor Statistics, Consumer Price Index – Food Away from Home (Series CUUR0000SEFV).

Bibliography

Allen, Nafeesah. "How to Start Investing in Index Funds." Investopedia, August 17, 2023. https://www.investopedia.com/how-to-start-investing-in-index-funds-5183569.

Executive Order 6102. "Requiring Gold Coin, Gold Bullion and Gold Certificates to Be Delivered to the Government." April 5, 1933.

Fidelity Investments. 2017 Millionaire Outlook Study. Boston: Fidelity Investments, 2017.

Federal Reserve Act of 1913. Public Law 63-43, 38 Stat. 251 (December 23, 1913).

Huff, Darrell. How to Lie with Statistics. New York: W. W. Norton & Company, 1954.

Kiyosaki, Robert T. Rich Dad Poor Dad: What the Rich Teach Their Kids About Money That the Poor and Middle Class Do Not! New York: Warner Books, 1997.

Marks, Howard. Mastering the Market Cycle: Getting the Odds on Your Side. Boston: Houghton Mifflin Harcourt, 2018.

Popham, Lauren, Susan Silberman, and Liz Berke (National Council on Aging), and Jane Tavares and Marc Cohen (LeadingAge LTSS Center at UMass Boston). The 80%: The True Scope of Financial Insecurity in Retirement. Washington, DC: National Council on Aging, May 2020.

Ramsey Solutions. The National Study of Millionaires. Franklin, TN: Ramsey Solutions, October 3, 2024.

SmartAsset. What Percentage of Retirees Have a Million Dollars? SmartAsset, March 25, 2025. https://smartasset.com/retirement/what-percentage-of-retirees-have-a-million-dollars.

Soforic, John. The Wealthy Gardener: Life Lessons on Prosperity Between Father and Son. New York: Portfolio/Penguin, 2020.

Stanley, Thomas J., and William D. Danko. The Millionaire Next Door: The Surprising Secrets of America's Wealthy. Atlanta: Longstreet Press, 1996.

U.S. Const. amend. XVI (1913).

U.S. Congress. Employee Retirement Income Security Act of 1974. Pub. L. 93–406, 88 Stat. 829.

www.ingramcontent.com/pod-product-compliance
Lightning Source LLC
LaVergne TN
LVHW100300210926
848480LV00003B/982
* 9 7 9 8 8 9 6 9 4 7 2 6 4 *